Question. How do you pack a mountain of inspiring, life changing wisdom into 90 pages? *Answer.* It is not difficult, if your name is C.Rebecca. In the *Art of Forgiveness*, C.Rebecca not only tells her own 'warts and all' story, but with frankness openness and skill rarely seen, she shares the struggles, failures and successes of her life journey, and in the telling, empowers the reader by sharing the principles and values that once applied, led to her personal transformation.

The story will leave the reader wondering where she discovered the wisdom, that added a richness to her life, even as she was struggling to survive in the darkest and most difficult of times. Such wondering will be rewarded in the last chapter.

The Art of Forgiveness is a 'must read, for those who need healing and for those who care for them.'

Graeme C. Cann, Warrigul Church of Christ

C. Rebecca bares her emotions, her soul, her life! She's not for holding back, as she traces the depths of her personal trauma and self-discovery, with surprising vulnerability. But it's C. Rebecca's authenticity that draws us in as guests on her journey into the hard-won freedom she's experienced through forgiveness. This liberty isn't cheap, but costly! Yes, this story is replete with skills and activities the reader can adopt to identify and confront injustice and challenges. However, it's C. Rebecca's continuing tenacity for personal transformation over many years, that most deeply challenges readers to the deep-level attitudinal change crafted and empowered by Love. Love seeks the ultimate best for all involved. Love is a decision!

Ian L Grant PhD, Christ-follower, Intercultural Leadership Coach, Missiologist, Pastor

Don't pause in the dark. That is how C. Rebecca explains it as you read her very personal memoir about forgiveness. After all, forgiveness is something that deeply affects everyone. No one is exempt from wrestling with the reality of forgiving someone who has deeply wounded them. And we just get stuck in our pain, indignant at the injustice of our suffering. We pause in the dark.

But in the midst of her overwhelming anguish, she discovered how freedom must become your focus and your goal. Freedom from the past and freedom for yourself because we were designed to be free. C. Rebecca's journey will help you not to pause in the dark, giving you hope, pointing you towards real freedom.

Greg Murray

The Art of
Forgiveness

C. Rebecca

Gold-Crested Press
Beaconsfield, Victoria 3807, Australia

Gold-Crested Press is the quality self-publishing imprint of Cardinia Ranges Publishing House enabling, through quality-guarantee and distribution, independent authors to inspire people.

cardiniaranges.com

The Art of Forgiveness
Copyright ©2023 by C. Rebecca
First published 2023

ISBN: 978-1-922537-18-8 (Paperback)
ISBN: 978-1-922537-19-5 (EPUB)
ISBN: 978-1-922537-20-1 (Kindle / Mobi)

A catalogue record for this book is available from the National Library of Australia

NATIONAL LIBRARY OF AUSTRALIA

Table of Contents

Table of Contents

Introduction

*F*orgiveness. What an interesting, frustrating, and rewarding act.

Learning and receiving from multitudes of resources, along with various friendships and relationships, I uncovered the importance and value of acting in forgiveness. I witnessed and embraced many of the hurting individuals around me. This highlighted my struggles of hurt and grief. I lived with heartbreak and trauma while continually posing a carefully guarded exterior. I pleaded with myself to find a place of peace. I longed to fast-forward, to overcome reoccurring hurdles, to reach the other side that I knew would offer freedom and happiness. I wanted so much more than just to survive.

Throughout *The Art of Forgiveness*, I hope to walk you through some thoughts and concepts that I encountered while endeavouring to forgive and to gain deeper insight into forgiveness. As you begin this book, I ask you to open your mind a little more than it is now.

On the cover, there is a picture of a *Kintsukuroi* art piece. This, in so many ways, is symbolic to me of what forgiveness can represent. The artwork is Japanese, and it is a repair of broken pottery with powdered gold, silver, or platinum, mixed with lacquer to glue the pieces together. I share this artwork with you because there is beauty when something broken and insignificant is brought back together and restored strategically. Forgiveness is like the beautiful and precious lacquer that brings relationships back together. Instead of disregarding someone or something in life that has hurt or betrayed us, we can choose to pick up the broken pieces and strategically repair what has been lost.

There is so much delight when people live in freedom and love freely, after such grief and rejection. This artwork is a physical manifestation of resilience and restoration. This beauty is not always observed from the outside (like an art piece) but from the inner well-being that shines through the exterior. The emotional heart can repair, restore and find the freedom to live with trust and happiness again. This process becomes evident over time, and I can truly say I have observed the benefits of forgiveness in action.

Refusing to forgive can dampen the positivity that encapsulates a person's heart, holding them prisoner to the pain. I experienced this and it was excruciating. I struggled to maintain everyday habits, and chores, to have relationships, and to be effective, let alone stay positive in any way. Everything became too hard, and I recognised I was stuck there. The motivation to break free came from the need to be free. Life was horrible being a captive. I pushed forward, trying to find ways to chip away at this prison I was locked in.

The name of the book represents the process. I believe for-giveness is an art. In the initial stages of the Japanese artwork, a completed pottery piece is brought before the craftsman. It is beautiful. Just like the process of forming pottery, we will journey through our growth stages, exhibiting our unique qualities and individualism. Yet some kind of tragedy can occur that painfully breaks our world apart. During these uncontrollable occurrences, many negative emotions can surface and a dark place for unforgiveness can grow.

I think of the next step in creating the *Kintsukuroi* art, and how the craftsman breaks the pottery into pieces. The original art piece can no longer serve its purpose and should be discarded. With this in mind, we have the choice to process the circumstances that have hurt us incredibly. We can move forward with more resilience and strength than before.

Coming back to the art piece, the resealing of the pieces of pottery with divine materials will bring forth more artistry and exquisiteness. This process of art was a strategic move of the craftsman. We also may have circumstances that are beyond our control, that seem to destroy our original life, our original function. Why not proactively process these moments in life, so that our lifestyle can truly move in a direction with more strength, freedom, and love?

Progressing through the various stages of forgiveness can be tiresome, stretching, and hard work. However, the rewards can last a lifetime. Knowing how to forgive and to let go is a beneficial process for everyday life. It can truly free a person and restore them to their true self, with a positive mindset and hope for a future of blessed relationships. Not only will I share moments of brokenness, hurt, and despair but I hope to share the steps that I learned to overcome these dark places in my life and to empower you to apply such acts or disciplines. I have seen the value of forgiveness as my life progressed in freedom from hurt and brokenness. I understand the struggle to even consider the choices in this journey, but friend, please hear me when I say this: *You can do it.*

After the broken pieces of pottery are brought back together with the lacquer, time and pressure are taken to set the lacquer. This hardening process allows the broken pieces to stay sealed together, assembling a unique creation that was once broken but now is restored. Forgiveness, when chosen and applied, needs the time and the circumstances to be sealed. This book will journey through examples of this process of choosing to forgive, applying forgiveness at every turn, and remembering that forgiveness has released all involved.

I hope to openly and honestly share parts of my journey with you. It involves heartbreak, progressive hardship, and continuous growth, with the various lessons learned to overcome anxiety, depression, and how to forgive. I have had the privilege of speaking with many women and men about their journeys of heartbreak, broken relationships and loss. I have gained insight into the human heart and the emotions that revolve around forgiveness. Though the last number of years has been challenging, the rewards have been greater. I have seen the power of forgiveness through relationships, and how it creates unity, freedom and peace. I have seen how wise counsel has encouraged and guided me through the torment, and of releasing overwhelming feelings and emotions that had darkened my everyday life.

Though this story initially has a dreary introduction, I would love to share the keys learned through facing the adversity caused by poor choices and the freedom received from releasing uncontrollable circumstances. The idea that forgiveness "lets the other off the hook", or that "they get away with it", has been something that many have grappled with, including myself. However, the ongoing liberation of forgiveness and pursuit to find peace despite the crazy chaos that surrounds our minds is achievable with a daily proactive process and choice. Sometimes, I catch myself thinking did this happen to me? I have come to a place of true forgiveness, and therefore, I can have positive relationships with the other parties involved. I no longer hold onto anything from the past and this has been repeated to me over and over again by friends and family who have witnessed it.

By writing these thoughts down about my story and what I have learned, I am again faced with the past, and how powerful forgiveness was for me. I have been set free of horrible memories and bitterness, I hold no negativity or regret towards the other parties involved, and I no longer have issues with my health. I have hope again for love and I live a life of contentment and peace. I believe we can all achieve this place of freedom and happiness, but the choice is ours to make. We choose to stay angry, to focus on the dreadful circumstance, and to allow the hurt to rip deeper into our hearts; or we can choose to be free. I can hear the inner voice fighting using these words: "*No*. It hurts. I have been wronged. I deserve justice. They deserve to suffer." But the focus is still on the circumstance and them, and not on releasing ourselves from the hurt. The focus should be on achieving complete freedom.

Like with a marathon, we can train our hearts and minds to take on this healthy discipline of forgiveness and achieving freedom. The process of forgiveness is like the training for the marathon. The finish line exists in the relationship resolutions as well as the freedom achieved from hurt.

When you start training for a marathon, it is hard on your body and mind. You have to be disciplined and determined to work the outer body (the muscles, joints, ligaments), and discipline on working the inner body (the lungs, heart, metabolism). For a marathon, you have to work daily, eat responsibly, sleep well, and exercise correctly.

At first, your body is sluggish, it finds it hard, you wake up sore and hungry, and unmotivated. The discipline applied will help to motivate you and bring every muscle into order–the more you exercise, eat and sleep well, the more your body adapts to this way of life. The body responds more and more to the training you give it. Even when things slow down, the body is adjusting and engages in the change. Perseverance is key to seeing the finish line.

Before you know it, the pain dissipates, your cravings die off and you adjust to eating, sleeping, and working out a certain way. Eventually, you can run the marathon confidently because you have trained and prepared. Again, there is an art in training for a marathon, like creating an art piece and now, acting in forgiveness.

So, I compare the training for a marathon to the steps of progression to forgive. You have to work daily on disciplining your body, mind, and heart to let go of those hurtful memories and any trauma. The focus on forgiveness regains freedom to be your true self and to continue building healthy relationships.

The process initially is hard. Our body is sluggish to respond when repairing any relational betrayal. It is really easy to run away, rather than to bravely confront our feelings and proactively mend the relationship that once was beautiful.

Ideally, if there were no wrongs, relationships would be happy and in full function. Remembering that love and relationships are the goals, we endeavour to break through the frustration and pain, to gain stronger relationships. We also focus on the release of hurt, as this pain can imprison us into a negative space consisting of anger, frustration, guilt, shame, etc. These aspects will be discussed further and in more detail.

Let us remember what we are fighting for: a friend, love, and freedom. We need to be motivated and determined in resolving what has been lost or to release what is holding us back. We need to shut the doors of trauma and hurt with the force of forgiveness, and never look back. We need to move forward in freedom. Let us find the freedom to love and the freedom to live.

I want this for you, dear friend, to live in freedom and to be capable to love again.

Without further ado, I ask that you remember that this is only a snippet of my learning journey of forgiveness through the lens of a broken marriage and various other examples. I am still learning, and I hope to continue to learn for the rest of my days. I also ask that you take all that helps you or encourages you to be a step closer to freedom and peace, and disregard that which is not helpful in your journey. I hope that you find freedom, peace and joy, if you have not already found these in your life.

Thank you for stepping into this story and all the best with your journey.

Chapter 1
Why Forgiveness

Why should I forgive...?

Why give any care in the world about anyone else if they have purposefully hurt you? Why write an entire book about this concept of forgiveness?

Why consider forgiveness and the thoughts of another person, when they have no idea what I have been through? What is it about forgiveness that is so important, anyway?

Is letting go of the hurt and anger really going to help me? How can I move forward if the other party is not aware of the hurt that they caused me, or if justice has not been served yet? When should I forgive–can it wait? Or should I do it straight away, so that I can be hurt all over again?

Well, maybe I do not want to choose to forgive. Maybe I deserve to see justice, to be avenged, to perhaps see them suffer as I had. Maybe I just want them to understand, to grasp how deep the ache goes in my heart. Maybe it is too hard. I can picture someone poking their tongue out and chanting, "Nana-nana-na! I don't have to!". Or the angry emoji with symbols across the mouth. Or someone clicking their fingers and saying, "I don't have time for that!" I have heard multiple people speak their minds about forgiveness, or why they shouldn't forgive, mostly sharing their raw and fresh wounds of anger and frustration.

Seriously, what is so *important* about forgiving someone?

I can think of many stories, but I'll share this one. I started a new job and hoped to exemplify all of my skills with excellence.

However, only a few days into the role, I accidentally fed a laminator with two laminator sheets instead of one, abruptly halting the flow of the machine and almost breaking it. I felt my face flush and my heart jump, as it began to race quickly. I had to pull out the plastic sheets that were all crinkled and unusable, starting over. It felt like a painfully long time as I carefully pulled and pulled until the sheets were free. I apologised to the owner of the laminator and, to my surprise, they trusted me to use it *again*.

I was grateful for the mercy that they showed me with a machine that would have cost a few hundred dollars to repair (money that I did not have). I was also grateful for the trust they freely gave after the mistake. It made me think about the character of my colleague and the value of having their trust at work.

Another time, when I was young, I incredibly loved tiny ornaments or tiny trinkets that I could add to my collection. One night we visited a family friend's house and I saw a tiny book displayed through the windows on their enclosed bookshelf. I loved it, I wanted it, so I took it. We went home and I held onto that little book as if it were my most prized possession.

The next day my parents asked me if I had been making good choices the day before, and I immediately began to worry. I knew what they were referring to as the shame and guilt had been growing overnight. Continuing quickly, they asked if I had taken anything that did not belong to me. I initially insisted that I had been making good choices, but eventually I told them the truth about taking something that was not mine.

I sheepishly went back to this family friend's home that night and they asked me if it was right to take something that was not mine. I remember the feeling, of *knowing* that it was wrong as the sweat formed on my hands and face. There was a blush on my cheeks and a warmth fluctuating all over my body. As I nervously produced the book with tears swelling in my eyes, I repeated how sorry I was over and over. They hugged me and accepted my apology. They forgave me.

Why was forgiveness given when I had stolen an item, or almost broken an expensive thing? I believe I did not *deserve* forgiveness, even though I was a child or an adult who made a silly mistake. Now, these are things that can be easily resolved but those people had to overcome the initial anger and shock of almost losing something special or of value to them, and then remember that the individual in front of them was still learning.

When I purposefully or accidentally made mistakes and used my words to hurt my friends/family or when I lied/cheated/stole… The list of my wrongs is long and so is the list of my reasons for these mistakes: I was learning, hurting, influenced, naughty, human, you name it. Regardless the reasons, it was I who had made these mistakes; I caused the hurt to others. I was the one who let people down, hurt them, and betrayed them, and I know it did not deserve forgiveness. Yet most of these people forgave me. Why?

Following on, there was a time I was playing snooker with friends and family, and my family deduced from previous games that for me to win the game, they had to push all my buttons (at any cost). I remember the anger rising inside of me, the heated crimson flush in my cheeks, and my breathing starting at an irregular pace. In sheer determination, I would sink all the snooker balls into the holes. I would glare at whoever was taunting me, with fumes escaping my head in all directions. To see the look on their faces was sometimes enough to calm me right down.

I was not always so controlled; I would blow up and yell back hurtful comments not holding back in any way. The words directed at me were piercing and cruel, and the ones that came out of me were just as bad. I had to make a choice every time to let the words go.

When there was no chance of calming down, my dad would take me aside and remind me that (though it was not right), I could not control anyone and their responses. I could only control myself.

I could only control myself.

I was the one who needed to overcome my negative experience and be a victor amongst the adversity. Those words never left me. When bullies at school hurled nasty comments about my skin tone or my choices, beliefs, and lifestyle, I remembered the words my dad told me, I can only control myself and my response.

When friendships broke down for no reason, when various adults used manipulative language to control my circumstances and hurt my inner self, and when criticism was given without love or care, I would remember the words my dad had said and make a healthy choice for myself, to let it go. This was forgiveness every time.

At a young age, I realised what unforgiveness did to people. It *broke* people. It isolated them. It caused behaviour that was scary and unmerited. It separated the person from their true self. Unforgiveness robbed people of their happiness. It held them in a place of anger, resentment, and eventually, bitterness, hate, and becoming bad natured. It was hard to be around people like this, they seemed to be alone a lot of the time or otherwise they would repel their friends and family.

This sounds quite harsh, but I witnessed this response multiple times as a child, and now even more as an adult. It is very sad.

Unforgiveness, I feel, immobilises people's emotional state and ability to live a free and happy life. This lack of grace breeds contempt for anything or anyone who exhibits even a bit of the behaviours previously engaged with. The actions that follow can be detrimental to future friendships and relationships, sadly isolating the hurting person and sometimes destroying connections for good.

So again, why should we forgive? Hopefully, throughout this book, you can find a reason. Hopefully, you can come to terms with yourself as to why forgiveness is so vital to our health and well-being, and how necessary it is for living freely and contently with others.

One last point here. Growing up, my best friend was my brother. We were so alike yet so different. We aggressively fought, with emotions raging, and we gut-wrenchingly cried and boisterously laughed many times, all the while we were adventuring together.

There were thousands of fights and sometimes they were really bad. For those of you who had siblings, you would understand how the entire household felt tense from the sharp-tongued arguments and pin-drop silence. However, I can still clearly remember how our fights would come to an end. I don't remember how the fights started or what the content of the fight was, but interestingly I do remember how we resolved them. My brother or I would be tiptoeing around each other, trying to ignore one another, until finally one would give up with a burst of laughter...

Yes, *laughter!* It was like we found it hilarious that we were holding on to something trivial and trying to avoid each other while trying to rub it in each other's faces.

It was almost comical; but because of this laughter, something shifted. Like the heaviness of the hurt was lifted and all we could do was laugh out of utter joy that this weight was no longer dragging us down. The other person involved, whether my brother or I myself, would also immediately start laughing, and then the tears and hugs would come.

We would hug and apologise and specifically speak about forgiveness with each other. We would discuss all the details of what had led us to that point of anger, and how we could ensure a resolution was met quickly so that the argument would never need to occur again. This process may have been simplified most of the time, but these steps were taken to find a resolution.

Why did this become our practice? Because we value our relationship and friendship far more than being right or proving the other wrong, or even receiving justice. It shifted our approach every time moving forward. We loved each other more than the desire to be right. Sacrificial love is thinking of others before ourselves.

The act of forgiveness graciously saved many of my relationships, helping all of us on both sides to love, trust and live life together again. It created space for growth and freedom, for deeper friendships and relationships.

Every relationship is going to face highs and lows, joys and sorrows, especially if the relationship is mutual giving and receiving. No doubt, there will be conflict, and depending on the person, the relationship can either grow or grow apart, eventually becoming non-existent. Forgiveness should be a part of every growing relationship, almost acting like superglue when things fall apart. It can be artfully worked through life, intricately lacing in and out of circumstances and adventures of time. I hope to explore this idea with you in more depth throughout this book, with this we will be venturing into some of the hardest moments in my life, *but also how I got through it because of forgiveness.*

Part 1
Glazed

Chapter 2
Appearances

*B**e respectful. Be lady-like. Be quiet.*

Appearances play a huge role in everyday life. When attending a job interview, how you look, behave, and speak matters. Working in any career may require a uniform or dress code, and a code of conduct. In any form of leadership, your example sets a benchmark for others to follow. On a date, the features of a person are what initially attract the two people together. Appearances on the street could initiate a friendly smile and a hello, or cause repulsion, or aggravate or scare someone. There is so much weight in how a person appears, not only in looks but how they hold themselves, behave, and act in circumstances. Mostly, we are quick to judge according to appearances, sadly losing out on knowing incredible human beings because of it.

I think of a time when I was working as a dental nurse. It was late in the afternoon, finishing time was about thirty minutes away, and the clinic was running an hour behind schedule. It was a tiring day, and we would continue after hours. Patients were stressed throughout the day and vented their frustrations on the nurses. My own patience was nearing its end.

A gentleman had been waiting for about an hour now and he angrily approached the desk as I was trying to quickly complete payments for another patient. In an annoyed tone, he hastily asked me when he would be seen. I empathetically replied that we would see him as soon as we could. When another patient went in before him, he became very angry and told me off, saying that it was not good enough. He stormed out of the clinic.

I was initially shocked at his outburst and to be honest, a little agitated, but I understood. In fairness, I just wanted him to know that I could do nothing to change the circumstances. It was unfair to him to be waiting so long, but it was also unfair for him to be angry at me and treat me that way.

I thought about what I should do, whether or not I should have called him out on his behaviour. I spoke to the dentist, and he reminded me that the patients are already in a place of pain or hurt, they were frustrated for waiting for their appointment time and for being held over time, in their suffering.

Then, the dentist went a step further. He highlighted that we do not always know what else the person is going through in their personal life.

Now I was grateful that, even though I was annoyed and was losing my resolve, I had held my professional expectations and appearance intact. I was accountable and responsible for my actions, not others' responses to circumstances. I could respond with respect, empathy, and kindness. I could treat people how I would like to be treated. I reminded myself that as a nurse in the medical industry, we are required to care for and support the patient in need.

Thankfully, I had held my professionalism in place, despite being hurt for something I had no control over. I was grateful that I had asked for guidance rather than jumping into a verbal fight that would have helped no one. Though the situation could have been handled better, I am glad I kept my mouth shut. Especially given what the backstory was to this gentleman's anger.

When that patient eventually returned for his appointment days later, I was not there. The dentist apologised for the last encounter and for our clinic running so far behind in time. The dentist hoped he was feeling more positive this time around.

What happened next still shakes me to my core today. The gentleman shared that a few days before that appointment, he had lost his entire family to the tsunami that occurred in Indonesia. His *entire* family. They all travelled for a family gathering and he delayed a few days to have his sore tooth treated. He was supposed to join them on the weekend.

My heart broke for this man. He probably barely cared about the dental appointment. He most likely was trying to find function after such a huge tragedy had turned his world upside down. I recognised how important appearances are, but also how they can deceive us. I had no idea what he was processing or what he was even going through.

Maintaining appearances can be both rewarding and damaging. Through this example, I saw that a man completely broken on the inside could barely control *his* interactions with others. I also recognised I could maintain control of my own professional demeanour and actions. How different we were in circumstances and feelings, yet we both were trying to achieve control of our appearance.

So many people are expected to control their appearance, whether it is professional, emotional, or spiritual. This expectation can create negative spaces for unhealthy façades and loneliness in living life. People struggle to share their emotions in healthy ways, or through positive environments that can provide growth and support. Noticeably, people avoid support in fear of appearing weak, vulnerable, or out of control. This is detrimental to the well-being of any person.

With hope, I believe our present world is improving its understanding and outworking of support to the inner health and well-being of individuals. Appearances are important, but that does not in any way mean that they are complete. The factors that play vital roles for each person individually reside internally, mentally, socially and emotionally, not just outwardly in how someone looks physically.

Human beings do not always have to have everything together and I would like to keep reminding all of us that it is OK to not be OK. I share about appearances and expectations because we all have them. It can be hard to admit we need help, but it is OK.

Support can help us grow beyond detrimental or tragic situations. Support can enlighten us about things we do not see or know. It can be the pillar of strength (or the ounce of strength) we need to get up again. I know that I have leaned on multiple areas of support already throughout my life. I am *super* grateful for them all and pray blessings over them continually.

I have been teaching my son that he is not alone and that he can have support at any time; it is not a weakness. There are many avenues of support, even if we have encountered negative sources, there is always hope.

Friend, if you need help, it is OK. You do not need to work at anything alone. You do not have to have all the answers or hold appearances when you are breaking inside. Reach out for help. *It is OK to not be OK.*

Chapter 3
A Glimpse into the Past

*C*ulture is an integral part of our everyday existence, whether we like it or not. Culture births concepts and views that are taught from infancy, and outwork into society creating mixed traditions. Sometimes it can be hard to understand what is acceptable and what is true.

I was raised to live a certain way and, though I appreciate it, I know that I learned to adapt early. I grew up in a strictly conservative home. As a female, I would have to behave and dress a certain way: nothing above the knees, nothing that showed any curves or body parts. Clothes were thrown away if they were too fitting or short. I had no choice in what I could wear to camps, birthdays, or events.

It was expected that the child respected their parents, followed their direction, and would behave honourably. We were not allowed to be moody or have bad attitudes, and conversations about expectations followed if this occurred. I appreciated this sense of discipline as I learned quickly to respectfully control my responses to situations, to adapt if needed, or to respectfully speak up and hope for change.

Throughout my life, I was told what a good woman "looked" like. A good woman would keep a positive and joyful household, maintaining it clean and tidy. She would keep her home warm, lovingly providing a welcoming environment before thinking of herself. She was a cook, making every belly joyful and content. She would be praised for her ability to construct incredible meals that would bring others to the table.

I was also taught that a good woman is submissive to her husband. To follow him and encourage him, being ready to help him at any time.

In my all-girls high school, the message communicated from the top offered an alternate view of what a good woman looked like. The principal at the time spoke highly of her independence and feminist views of living equally as a woman in current society.

She shared the endless possibilities of education and career. She highlighted that family is not for everyone and that having children does not make you a successful woman. She even communicated that a woman does not have to cook or clean and that they can pay for others to do so.

She seemed to target *me* with these views.

On reflection, it was my inner recognition of who I could be, despite my cultural upbringing. The battle raged in my mind of what was acceptable, honourable, and pleasing to my family, to culture, to society, and to me.

It was difficult for me to be told that I could not do certain things because of my gender or because it was not safe for me. I realised I had some apprehension towards the future as well as frustration for the limitations placed on me as a female.

When I completed school, my principal spoke directly to me saying, "You can do anything a man can do, and do it even better. Don't allow anyone to stop you from living up to your fullest potential. You are made for so much more than rearing children and becoming a good housewife."

I agreed with her partially, but also believed in balance, not extremes.

It was not negative to be a whiz in the kitchen and to create meals that made mouths water. It was not wrong to be clean and maintain a beautifully clean household. I think that I was grappling with the culture I had lived with *versus* the society I live in. I had to come to terms with what was acceptable to me; after all, I was living this life.

I set out trying to find balance, taking positive points of view from both cultures and releasing the negative points of view that would hold me back. I wanted to live free and happy, fully embracing who I was; the individualistic, dreamer, female. I had to let go of the things that were holding me back.

Moving forward, for any teenager seeking out a career can be challenging, but I was seeking out a path that would be helpful and rewarding to the community. I wanted to be a teacher and join the staff at my local church, though I have to admit that these were not the highest-paying career choices. Teaching, to me, seemed so rewarding and had benefits for the future, while my heart wanted to help people in need through the church. My family was accepting the changes in who I was and how I desired to live life, acknowledging that I was living for a purpose, not a reward, though I believe they intertwine remarkably. The culture of my family was shifting to accept equality in the home while honouring the culture of my parents' past. The encouragement to follow my dreams while fulfilling responsibilities as an adult was set in motion.

However, the negatively geared conditioning in my life commenced about a year into dating my future husband. The urge to have a respectful job that provided for the family was pushed at us from both ends. This is true in one sense and those who loved us dearly needed to teach and guide us in this. Yet, the pressure of this seemed to cause more stress in our relationship, with the constant urgency to land a high-paying and respectable job.

Though I desired to work as a teacher, they kept telling me about options for other roles, because of a better income. I was often belittled in conversations around education, almost like it was not a good-enough career for our future endeavours. When I bought my first home, the pessimistic apprehension from these opposing parties eased a bit. I had done so at a young age on a part-time wage while studying and this proved that some of the negative points for taking a teaching job were incorrect. I found, however, that cynical comments still trickled into my ears, breaking any sense of achievement.

When I completed my degree, and my apprenticeship, and landed my dream job, I was met with negativity and disdain. The remarks of "You could do better than that," or, "This worked for me, change it so it could better your outcomes," and "There's always room for improvement," always dampened any positive emotion within. With constant negativity around any achievements, it became hard to share with the opposing family members and friends anything that had happened at work, with study, or with my friends and family. The problem was not offering advice or constructive criticism, rather it was the lack of acknowledgment of the good work or achievement, or the effort I had put in. It was the constant nagging of this negative pressure that broke my spirit over and over.

It was only after I had married and subsequently separated, that I realised the negativity inflicted upon me was the product of the own fixed expectations, control, low self-esteem, and lack of value from these opposing parties themselves. However, the damage had already been done and had taken its effect.

I had begun to believe that everything I did was not good enough and that I was not worthy of the blessings and relationships around me. I would defend my husband to everyone (parents, bosses, friends) thinking that he was totally or near to perfect; that he could achieve anything. The belief system within me had formed to protect and nurture him, and to belittle myself as I was not good enough for him. I was never going to measure up to what he wanted, but I would always try to because I loved him.

Honestly, I believed that men deserved more than women; I resented being a woman and began to hate what I had become. Though I had education about equality and the rights of women, I now can attest to how vital positive and constructive communication is needed in putting these values into action; not only for one gender but for all.

I believed that I was less deserving than the man I married. I believed I should serve him and simply accept his lack of affirmation or contribution. I had started to allow the control and negative treatment to become my everyday lifestyle.

I had undone all that positive work of balancing my cultures from my past and current lifestyle by taking on this negative mindset. I had completely accepted this treatment and lifestyle as my norm, and in the process lost the woman I had been developing into. This had happened gradually and started before I was married, and all too subtly. People who witnessed this series of events brought them to my attention, but I was too stubborn or proud to accept the help. I desired my relationship so much that I sacrificed my own freedom and compromised my values.

I share this, because sometimes we compromise ourselves for those we love, or we just want to keep the peace. Speaking about differences should be a normal part of our journey, as we are unique in personality, beliefs, and upbringing. We are similar but also radically different, and I think this is fantastic! We were made to be us: individual, precious, and wonderfully made. I was made to be me, and you were born to be you. Yes, compromise is a part of life, but we should never lose ourselves or stomp out our lights. We are meant to shine in *our individual personalities.*

Chapter 4
Marriage

*A*s *you become more comfortable* with someone, they allow their flaws or true personality to shine through. This happens after you pass through the honeymoon phase of a relationship, a time of continuous giggling and PDA or "public displays of affection" overwhelming everybody and where you tend to spend hours with one another and no one else.

But then, reality kicks in. You begin to argue a little, or a lot; you have multiple differences and call each other out on these, every time. The frustration builds when you can no longer have free time to play sports, see other friends independently of each other, or know what's appropriate with the opposite gender. The list can be ever-growing if there isn't grace.

I know that in current times it can be easy to say "bye" to people who are not encouraging or building towards a life of commitment. It can be easy to walk away even after a honeymoon phase of many years and enjoy nothing deeper than superficial gratification. I think a commitment to another person can cause fear, repulsion, and even break down a beautiful relationship because of what comes with this act. Commitment says that even if you are wronged by love, you choose to love and fight for the relationship. "Nothing will separate us because I am committed to this."

I am the type of person to make a choice and follow it through. With my partner, my choice was covered in commitment to him, from the depths of my heart. With or without a honeymoon period of loving, I was all in.

Surely, when negativity flowed out of my partner's mouth, I accepted it and tried to use it to better myself. I believed that he desired growth for both of us, that he had a vision in mind and went about applying it the way he knew how, even though he expressed it harshly.

Communication between us began to deteriorate progressively because the goal was always to succeed, always to be better, without acknowledging what we had already achieved. This is not necessarily a bad thing but for some personality types, but it can become negative, and the feeling of being pressured to change can stunt growth. I know that for me, I could not handle it all the time. Sometimes I just needed to hear: "Well done." Full stop. Nothing more.

Let me explain this. When I purchased my first home on a part-time wage, a few years out of school, most people would say: "Well done. What an achievement to purchase a home on your own, pretty much straight out of school."

However, in private, I was met with questions about the location of the home and how far away it was. I was told that I could have made a better choice, that it was an uneducated choice of location, and that I could have invested elsewhere. I remember thinking: yes, I could have; I wish I did! It was because I loved this man and was committed that I let these words break my sense of positivity and achievement.

Sometimes, though we have love and commitment for our loved ones, we still have to look at their example, how they live, spend their money and treat others. He came into our relationship with debts from unknown purchases and bills. I fully accepted this difference and did not hold it against him.

However, I had learned how to budget and to apply my finances to work for me, which made him feel insecure. These successful events, of finishing school and soon after buying a home, seemed to affect his self-esteem because he thought that he should be the provider. I saw us as a team from the start, but that did not matter to him. His belief system about himself progressed into negative behaviour that affected our relationship, marriage, and communication.

Unfortunately, this poor treatment only grew with time, as I began to complete degrees and take on my dream job. I tried to help him with his choices (study, work, church life) but his pride kept me at arm's length. I found that I could not do anything, as he was stuck in his private world, and I was bombarded with negative venting. I had no control over what he said or how he behaved, but it was always targeted at me.

On reflection, I can hear words of projection; though the accusations were targeting me, they were really about himself. For example, he would say, "You wanted a big wedding, so we have debt." However, we didn't even pay for our wedding, and my preference would have been to simply elope, anyway.

In this space of time, I found that I was trying everything to make him happy. I would buy him his favourite drinks and lollies, I would to help him study. I even thought of approaching family members or friends for help, but he became very upset if I would mention anything to them. I noticed that this pattern of behaviour had emerged that where I would freely chat with friends or family, I would be reprimanded later on in the car for saying something or doing something that he did not like. I started to believe that I was wrong every time. Sometimes, I would cry but he would say or do nothing; I was just left by myself to overcome my emotions.

What had started as a partnership had become a dictatorship. He would speak it and it would be done accordingly; or I would be met with manipulative comments to destroy my inner worth. This treatment progressed into control of everything that came in and out of our relationship.

I soon found that with my friendships before this relationship (especially with other men), he had a say in how I interacted with them. I was not allowed to hug them or greet them with a kiss on the cheek. I was told to maintain my distance and, somehow in the conversation, I had to bring him up, reminding them that I was with him. I respected this point of view, but I also found that he would not reciprocate this with female friends. I found that I was treated one way whereas he could behave another, basically however the way he wanted in that same scenario. Sometimes, it angered me enough that I would be silent for the rest of the night, but then I would be berated for how I was behaving. No matter what, I was always wrong. I could always grow. I could always be better. Nothing I did or said was ever good enough.

This caused me to escape internally into a shell of protection. I began to work at the suggestions with positivity and hope, but on the inside cowered and hid from the outside world. I was hoping to achieve greater things, to set us up for the future, and to be a better communicator. I applied myself even more than before, reminding myself continually that he loved me and only wanted me to grow.

However, I was waiting for him to say: "Well done." When he did, it ruled out everything else that had been going on. I could feel myself creep out of my protective shell to enjoy time in celebration but then would quickly creep back in, again. I desired positive acknowledgment, instead of a constant pessimistic view of life.

I had experienced this early on with my partner, but I chose to commit. I chose him. Now we were together, I had made this my life. I had to figure out how to positively live with his personality type and the actions that flowed from him. I would hear a saying repeat in my mind every time I was faced with criticism and control: "This is my lot in life."

There were wonderful moments, and we shared happiness in hobbies, friends, and going out. It just seemed that our goals in life were not clearly communicated to one another or seemed compromised and hidden, just in the hope that the other would change. Without healthy communication and finding common ground, the pressure and control started to accelerate.

You may be thinking, "How did you both stay in the relationship for so long?" Truthfully, I completely loved him, and we made the choice to commit. I was broken over the choice to end it, but there was so much wrong with us being together while dating. Many people in our lives had spoken up about this freely, and I finally listened. In fact, after the break-up, most people communicated their relief and encouraged me on the choice I had made to move forward.

To those of you who would have walked away, have walked away, or are about to walk away: despite the break-up, the treatment that I was conditioned to still had to be processed and released. This conditioning to control and manipulate can exist in life after bad relationships. We can allow control to destroy our very nature and well-being if we do not face it and overcome it.

I did walk away after things became dangerous, but I had to process so much after, especially the conditions of control and manipulation. I will get into this later, but I can honestly say to you, that even after danger had presented itself, I was willing to stay and blame myself.

Within the next year of singleness, I found it really hard to be alone. I thought that maybe I had made a mistake, but I decided to shut out the idea of going back to such a negative relationship. The conditioning of that lifestyle ultimately had begun to wear off and I finally started to believe that I was worthy of happiness and love again. It was about six months later that I started to have a healthy mindset and to dream again of great things. I started a new degree and began making better choices for my health and well-being.

The new me also began to catch the attention of my ex-partner as he recognised the woman again that he had fallen for years before. He started to chase after me *again!*

Now writing this, I can hear myself saying, "Don't do it."

Surprisingly, I restarted the relationship with this man after six to eight months of talking and working through the unresolved issues. I fully believed that we had worked through our issues and that we could now move forward to marriage. I trusted so easily and ignored any advice about working through any issues more deeply. I remember when we had pre-marriage counselling and how I felt throughout the sessions. I trusted every word my partner was saying because as for myself I *was* telling the absolute truth (embarrassing as this was). I believed that we were finally completely real and honest with one another and my entire trust and inner being went into this relationship.

As a side note, some people spoke their minds regarding our relationship, and my ex-husband and I did engage in multiple, heated discussions. I can remember the fiery arguments and my dense ignorance to the warning signs they were sharing. I was perfectly blinded because of the love I had and my fear of being alone. Others were too afraid to communicate their truths with me, because of their fear that I would fall apart. I admire both parties and only have heartfelt blessings for them.

Nevertheless, the milestones of life came very quickly after that, we were eager to get married and his family pushed for it. It was a little over a year after getting back together that we were married. Now, these were happy times, and we had a crazy busy year of preparation. My partner worked on making our wedding day reflecting us personally and respectfully declined traditional practices offered by both families. It was as stressful as always when you plan a wedding and include every family member and friend. The greatest concern that plagued my mind was simply to be accepted by him and his family.

I remember the morning of the wedding and how everyone around me could see that I was holding up a front. Words of concern and gentle urges to calm down and have something to eat or get dressed were communicated with delicacy. My best friend amusingly revealed how my shoulders relaxed after he said, "I do." I could picture someone objecting to our marriage, I suppose, and when that did not occur, I finally calmed. The day was joyful and complete with happy tears and roaring laughter.

Life went on, as we were always planning for the future and never stopping to be content, hoping for a bigger house and an even better job. The strive to be bigger and better never let up in our household. There was always this pressure of having to be the best; anything less was unacceptable. The conditioning, that I mentioned before, began again; very subtly at first. I was happy in my job and our home; truly I was content. I knew that with hard work and patience, the possibility for the next big step that we were hoping for was imminent.

My partner, however, was *not* happy; he had to travel quite a distance to work a job that he did not like. He was not content and made this clear countless times, sometimes alluding to me that it was my fault. It was my fault that I had chosen a house so far away from the city. My fault that I had chosen teaching: maybe a mediocre paying but still a respectable job.

We sold the house and moved. We were planning for children later, and we were working hard and saving our money, that was key. Unfortunately, he could not commit to his degree, therefore working hard in his job and making beneficial connections was the only way to work his way up the ladder. It was difficult because in the process he had to make some choices that did not line up with our values. I tried to partner with him, but he would not allow me to be a part of it. I think it was eating away at him as he became very negative and frustrated with life. Still, he would not talk about it and would angrily shoo me away if I ever tried to ask.

Throughout the years we were together, I was blaming myself for our situation. I was unsure if it was because of his words or because I believed I was the cause of his unhappiness, but I just tried to make him happy. I would persistently encourage him, placing myself second to his needs and desires. I tried to save money wherever we could, to give him a better experience with friends or holidays. I remember trying to spend the least amount of money on our weekly groceries, and every dollar less was an achievement. Our family finances he never shared with me, but still I trusted that he was managing everything well. He never let on that anything was wrong despite any questions I had around payments or bills. I worked hard to complete all household chores, including his; then, he could come home and just relax. I tried to create and cook better meals, though there was very little encouragement on his end.

It became increasingly harder as he would keep berating my efforts with negativity making me feel unworthy again. Sometimes he would belittle me in front of our friends and then laugh and say it was a joke. I felt like crying most of the time. I would be told off for retreating away from the conversation when I did. I remember one time when he began saying discouraging things making everyone laugh at me. I could not hold on any longer, so I excused myself and went to the bathroom and cried. I stayed there for a while until I had calmed down, cleaned myself up, and joined the conversation again. This may have gone unnoticed, but my quietness did not. Again, I was reprimanded for being withdrawn and unhappy.

This became a regular occurrence, unfortunately. Sometimes he would catch me tearing up or even silently crying, but then he would scoff in disgust. He would ask about what I was crying about now and would encourage me to find a way to overcome my issues if I didn't like it how he had been approaching them.

The negative treatment shifted when I found out that I was pregnant. It was like he had seen the light of his behaviour and began to respect my drive to bring a positive environment to our son. I worked full-time and saved everything I could to provide for the arrival of our baby. I was anxious about pregnancy, especially since it was my first child, and I would be one of the first in our friendship group to have a baby. The thoughts of what could be were very exciting but the negative thoughts and worries were there, too. I could not talk to my husband during this time as I was afraid that he would just belittle me or start treating me negatively again. About how I was physically feeling, I spoke regularly to the doctor and my mum, but I never spoke honestly about how I felt emotionally for fear of making my husband angry. Not that he would physically hurt me, but I was afraid that he would yell at me afterwards, like before, for including anyone in our private affairs or revealing what was supposed to be a family secret.

I had best friends visit regularly, so I used this time to take my mind off the weird and painful relationship I had with my husband. The idea of a baby coming into our family may have shifted the perspective in our home, and with the focus taken off me, of being the culprit, brought life in me again. I thought this was just a phase of difficulty within marriage and that we were simply like everyone else, seeing it through the best we can.

Marriage is between husband and wife, yet there was a lack of understanding on how to have a healthy marriage. There was no guidance or support when either person needed it, and now I see that hiding the struggle only damaged our relationship further. It is OK to seek help. Shame and guilt only hold us in a place of entrapment and lack of growth. If we truly love our partners, family and ourselves, we will seek out the trusted help and support we need to proactively process circumstances *and implement positive change.*

Part 2
Broken

Chapter 5
The Storm

*A*nticipation. Excitement. Sheer joy. Apprehension. Fear. Anxiety. With something new, comes a multitude of feelings. I was feeling so many different emotions when I understood that I was pregnant. We were not planning to have children so early, and yet, bubs were a pleasant surprise.

I had joked with friends in the past about having children and how I would opt for some procedure to avoid any pain. I had thought about the changes that would happen to my body, and how I would try to maintain a healthy physique.

I had spoken to multiple women about their pregnancies and labour stories, worked with babies and toddlers, and understood some of the responsibilities. Yet nothing could compare with becoming pregnant, having the changes occur within, and experiencing the miracle for myself.

My body began to feel different and change almost immediately, and, to my surprise, I knew I was pregnant. The confirmation of pregnancy both excited me and terrified me. I remember taking the test at work, having to hide the news from my workplace (my boss was my father, can you believe it?), and staying composed without giving anything away. It was interesting to work through the transformations in my body, both physically and internally with my hormones.

Initially, I was in shock. However, I also knew that this little being growing inside of me was a blessing and miracle from above. I really had to work on changing my thought processes to not only accept what was going on, but also to be overjoyed that I would soon have a baby.

Working on the mind, being positive, and saying "no" to fear was hard work. Every day, it became increasingly clear to me how important it was to acknowledge and accept the changes and to take steps closer to being a family. I needed to completely own this shift in lifestyle.

Every day, I would remember to be grateful for our good health, that we had a secure place to live and sufficient income; these are all so important in preparing for a family. I had been working full-time and I trusted that the money was going into a secure place for our family.

During my pregnancy, I was finding that I was tired a lot of the time and increasingly desired to have my personal space. Inwardly, however, something marvellous was happening to me: I was building a resilient and determined mentality that could produce a strong, perseverant and capable mother.

I was reading a lot of books about pregnancy and building positive mindsets and boundaries to better understand and benefit my impending motherhood. With this time of change and transformation, I also began to notice the change that was happening in my marriage.

Towards the last trimester of pregnancy, I started to notice that my husband's comments were becoming increasingly critical of me. Even more than before! It started with my cooking which would start a barrage of negative comments flowing at the end of the meals. This progressed into criticising me for the smallest things like every time I would flip something over in the pan or cut something at the table. There was always something wrong in the kitchen. I wanted it so much that I could be better at cooking! I would ask for his help, but he would then just say that it is food and that he'll eat it.

However, that did not stop the criticism. He would berate me time and time again in the car after going out with friends, because in his eyes I "was not friendly enough" or I "didn't smile or speak to someone that I was meant to." I would speak about something good that happened at work or with friends, and he would still find something to criticise. I would be told off on the way home after time with family because I "didn't offer to help with anything" so that he had to do it. However, they had actually asked me to relax and not to do anything, because I was pregnant.

This treatment had now become my reality, even though I thought we had worked on changing it already years before. And now, we were married with a baby on the way. He wanted to keep our relationship so private and surrounded it with so much secrecy, that I could not possibly speak to anyone about what was going on. To simply talk to someone could have saved our marriage, but somehow, along the way, I believed that this was everyday life in marriage and that this was *normal* and *acceptable*.

In my third trimester of pregnancy, to my shock, I also discovered that my husband was using pornography. For some this may not be a big deal, but for me it was really hurtful, and

I felt completely degraded as a wife, a woman, a human being. It was then that I felt a deep sadness occurring in my heart and I could no longer put up with his negative behaviour. After I had caught him, I initially couldn't do anything but simply cry. It took me a few days before I was able to speak up about what had happened, but then he would simply brush me off and highlight something else that he thought I needed to do. We never talked about it again, as he would stop any conversation that would lead to us discussing our intimacy.

So, with the knowledge that my husband was looking at other women and the continued criticism, I began to cower into a shell, into a protected, private and isolated world. Trying to remain positive for the baby, who was about to grace us with his presence, I chose to block out the painful negativity so that I could fully engage with motherhood and be positive about it.

Enter Matthew, beautiful and healthy. And, completely reliant on me as his drink bottle. This helped me finally find an escape from the negative relationship that had been pushing me further into my shell away from whom I used to be. I focused on being the best mother that I could ever be, knowing what to do when he cried, how to move from one growth spurt to the next and how to help him sleep well and effectively. Encouraging a routine around Matt also helped me to have a routine and general healthiness for myself. Six months passed very quickly, and, during this time, I had become so used to the criticism, that I thought things had settled between our family.

We then decided to go on an overseas trip together with my in-laws. As we were planning this trip others were beginning to realise that something was wrong. My in-laws consistently asked how my husband was and whether something was the matter with him. They wanted to donate money towards the trip, but he fought with the support to finance. I became curious and asked about where the money was going from both our pay and my maternity leave, but he scolded me for even asking. He said that *he* works in the bank, so *he's* got it.

However, his father became concerned and spoke to me discreetly. He explained that my income should actually be enough to support the household, so where had his income been going all this time? His income was decently higher than mine! I began to raise questions about some of these things, but I was soon met with an aggressive attitude of "how dare you ask me that?"

He would turn it around and place the blame for our financial pressure on me for having a child so early and for going through the private medical system, although he and his extended family had been insisting upon that. I started to think that our financial position was all my fault. I thought that we struggled with bills and groceries because I had a baby so early and comfortably. The blame was built up so extremely in my mind that I began to skip meals to save money, buy cheaper goods for our needs and use every dollar received for whatever my partner said that it was for. I budgeted every dollar for the week and saved as much as I could, which would then be taken for some unknown purpose. The words from my father-in-law continued to plague me, that the money is disappearing without explanation and that I *should* know something about it.

The trip was wonderful for Matt and me, as we met the extended family and were blessed by everyone there. I spent most of the days outside with Matt, exploring the gardens and produce on trees. It was a beautiful time, and I was fully accepted and loved. Matt's dad, however, was always in bed, always locked in the room away from all of us. He barely did anything unless it was to eat or when he had some duties with the family. By this time, I didn't mind that and enjoyed the space away with Matt and the people who cared and encouraged me.

It was so wonderful, that when we were leaving, I cried when we had to say goodbye to my in-laws, who were staying a little longer. It was like somewhere inside of me wanted to stay with them as I knew the value and love they had for me, and how I had felt safe.

Oh, how things would change.

It started right when we'd arrived back from our trip, a friend messaged me and told me that she had seen a photo of my husband with some other woman in a nightclub. She sent me the photo and, when I saw it, I was completely lost for words. My thoughts jolted to an immediate stop; it was like everything in me just froze.

The interesting thing is how this photo had come about. I had given up partying a long time ago, well before I was married. My friend, who showed me the photo, had been married with kids for many years and certainly had also given up that part of her life. For my friend to then come across this photo on a club website was just bizarre, and, I believe, had a purpose. This photo began my journey to recognise my own worth again and to set myself free.

Back to that situation, I simply could not leave this unspoken. My friend gave me the sound advice, and encouraged me, to be careful when approaching him. I did not think he would cheat on me, I told her firmly, but she again said to approach with caution and to stay savvy no matter what he said. This was extremely difficult for me, but I remembered that in the past, when another incident occurred with his female co-worker, my mother-in-law, his own mother, had advised me to confront him instead of running away. With this in mind, I calmly asked him about the photo, but he brushed me off by saying that this woman was just his boss. We had a direct discussion about why this photo was not OK, but he responded with an unfazed demeanour and moved on. I was furious and hurt but could not express any emotion; I think I was dumbfounded that this photo had happened and that he was OK with it.

From that moment on, I really became aware of how secretive he had become and how absent he had been in our household. I mean, I had seen it before, but now I really started to take notice of it. He would not let me access his phone or social media. He would come home late and leave early.

During this time, I found our phones were linked through the "find my phone" app that he had set up when we were first married. Through this, I found he would lie about where he was going. I didn't like "spying" on him, but he was not being honest and I couldn't live like that any longer. I started having dinner with my parents and his and began avoiding the negativity and hostility that he carried. Our finances would keep being drained the moment they went into the account, but I could not see where any of it was going, as it went straight into his private account.

About a month after the incident with the photo, I began to plan Matt's first birthday. As this little boy was my only beacon of hope, I really wanted to make it a special day. Of course, I would need funds to plan for this event, but my husband told me that we had no money for any of it. He would then tell me off for not working even though we had my maternity pay and additional casual pay coming into our bank account!

To still go ahead with my plans, I chose to save money around our grocery shopping.

I managed to put together the entire party, including beautiful but simple invites and a wonderful and delicious cake. I had friends come over to help me and encourage me; though things didn't work out perfectly they were coming together. Yet again, everything was met with criticism by my partner, and I must admit, I was being pushed toward my breaking point.

The day before Matt's birthday, my husband had taken the day off to look after Matt while I was busy baking and preparing all the decorations. However, he decided to go out early in the morning and he wouldn't come back till evening. Matt still happily played with my friends and me, while we were trying our hardest to make everything. When any of my friends would ask where Matt's dad was, I'd answer with a shrug and an "I do not know." Still, I could see the concern on their faces as I was trying my hardest to hold back my tears.

Crying had become commonplace to me. I'd silently cry in the shower or bed when he was asleep. I'd cry while driving to places or home.

The only times of peace and happiness were the moments when I was with Matt. It was breaking me to be with a man that seemed to hate me, and it was breaking my heart to know that there wasn't much of a marriage left.

Then finally it was time for Matt's birthday party. On the day, my two best friends and I did all the work of setting up the decorations, preparing the food and getting the cake ready. This time I did not ask for his help, I just wanted Matt's dad to be there by a certain time to celebrate his son's birthday with us. Matt was dropped off at that time, but his dad left. The party was halfway through when he would finally return and join us. Family and friends subtly kept asking whether everything was OK and whether something was wrong with him. At this stage, I could not answer them. I put on a brave face but understood that our problems were becoming transparent to the people that loved us most.

During and after the party, people praised me for how well the food and desserts had come out. They asked me for recipes and some even wanted me to plan their parties for the future. My friends encouraged me to cook more often for them, because to them everything was so delicious.

This was so different from any response I had received from my husband in my own marriage throughout the years. I didn't know how to respond but with indifference and numbness. Progressively, I became more and more unhappy with him.

Our wedding anniversary would come soon after the party, but we chose to have a quiet dinner at home. It was uneventful and the emptiness inside me grew larger. He suggested that we should get away from everything by ourselves and without Matt. I agreed that a time after Christmas could work. After all the negative treatment, it was very hard for me to be excited or motivated to go anywhere with him, alone.

During this same time, I received the news that I had received a job offer and I celebrated this with my friends. When they asked if I had called my husband, and I replied with a no, they knew something was wrong.

One of my friends stayed and waited with me until my husband would come home so that I could tell him. I was apprehensive about the praise my husband gave me. I was so unhappy with these circumstances; I wanted to escape. Over Christmas, this unhappiness became very evident; he again would tell me off for my introverted and apathetic behaviour. I remained silent and accepted the verbal abuse over and over, like it had been the norm.

We attended a wedding after Christmas, and I was happy that my husband was a part of the bridal party. I was all so tired, hurt and only a shell of the person I used to be, that celebrating anything was far from any of my capabilities. I had already been reprimanded for being "lost" over Christmas, I dreaded what could come at this wedding.

Before he left, he insisted that I should be with him for the entire wedding and that we should leave together. I remember that he pushed me to dress nicely and keep carrying a smile. He also wanted to make sure that after the official part I would come over to him and be by his side.

It was so hard for me to fake anything at this stage. However, that night, I tried my hardest to be positive and still enjoy the festivities. The couple was so happy, the joy in the room was contagious and dancing happened naturally. I even laughed so many times that night with various friends until my face was hurting. In this glimmer of joy and hope, I thought that perhaps things can turn around and change for our marriage.

Late in the evening, my husband did not want to leave yet and asked if he could continue to party with the boys. I agreed and thought that it was OK, but also said that I had to go home and relieve the babysitter. After all, it was already really late. I said goodbye to him and everyone else and I went home quickly. I was feeling really happy for both him and myself.

After about thirty minutes, however, the door opened and he walked in. He was furious and fuming, telling me off for leaving. So many colourful words followed. When he asked me to explain myself, I was exhausted and had no patience. I told him firmly that we agreed on him going and I said goodbye.

Not sure if it was the alcohol that had affected his memory or if the boys had just changed their minds; still he knew he was in the wrong and walked away. I was again so shocked, that I just tried to go to sleep and ignore it. The positive thoughts I'd had before were vanishing quickly.

When New Year's Eve approached, we had been invited to an event that I really did not want to attend. By this stage, I was done with the manipulative verbal abuse, the constant criticism and the plaguing negativity. I did not want to be around him or go anywhere alone with him anymore.

I agreed with myself that my new year was going to start with complete positivity and love: a new year for a new start. So, I was utterly content to be with Matt at home alone, and far away from him. Done.

This rigid response broke through whatever blockages that were present in our marriage. No longer was I trying to patch anything up; it was now evident that we both were completely unhappy, and I was not going to fake anything anymore.

He then cried and begged me to still come with him. He remorsefully explained how he'd felt the distance and asked me to give that night as something for us. I relented and went with him.

I have to admit, it was an enjoyable night, and he behaved respectfully and kindly. For one of the few times, I was not verbally abused or criticised on the way home.

The next day, however, he asked to speak to me. I sat down next to him. And then he finally said it.

"I've had an affair."

I was so numb to him and to everything that had come over me the past few years, that I accepted this news without a fight. I simply responded with, "I forgive you. This is terrible, but we can overcome it. We need to get help though."

He then cried and praised me for my grace and kindness. He even fell to my feet and hugged my legs. I, however, was so completely filled with utter shock that nothing was coming through. I had turned to ice. We just left it at that.

Already patterns of behaviour had formed around our marriage, our family time and our leisure. It was so easy to create emotional distance, I think it helped me live in the marriage for so long. But the news that he had been with someone else, that he had willingly broken our commitment and trust to one another, shifted my stance on how to act, respond and just be.

This change in me became evident to him when he was trying to interact or talk with me. Within a week, he would come home drunk and abusive. He let out slurred profanities. He yelled at me that it was all my fault, that I had checked out of the marriage, so he would do the same. He then demanded that I should leave the house, because he claimed that it was his.

It was so hard for me to respond to anything when there were no words, none left in me, only tears. He could only scoff at me, call me names and belittle any action I would take, before he would retreat to a room and lock the door. Thankfully, Matt was asleep most of these times, never coming between us when his dad would uncontrollably yell or verbally abuse me.

Just breathe. Breathe. You're alive. You're healthy-ish. You've been functioning remotely well, especially considering the lack of sleep and the fact that nothing seems to help this lost cause. Wide awake, despite the desire to rest and possibly dream of something better. Maybe afraid of the nightmares that have been plaguing the subconscious, waking with cries for help, and realising the sweat-soaked bedding was caused by the stress of the repetitive nightmares. Or knowing that nothing can remove the nauseating feeling that constantly remains throughout the day; food of all kinds had little to no appeal, to be frank. It is not the end of the world. Or is it? Could it be possible that losing someone with whom you'd pictured your entire life, is so gut-wrenchingly painful, that life feels like it's over?

It certainly feels that way, all over. It sounds exaggerated, it sounds so dramatic, but really… It is unexpectedly hard to move, though the sun reassuringly rises, creating magnificent shades of oranges, reds, and yellows. It feels incredibly hard to picture anything positive, anything worth pursuing or pressing forward. All the self-talk, encouragement, and affirmation fall on brick walls and bounces back. Perhaps, some words slither through the cracks and penetrate through to the softer and unprotected interior.

Hoping for a new day.

It was difficult to eat the food made with love and empathy or to talk about the day that was: full of challenging work, interesting people, and new experiences that came with a new job. Or, to fully commit to and openly share in any type of conversation, for that matter, with any human being. The only joy I could grasp was my baby boy; he physically and emotionally needed me and loved me completely, and desired a loving response. A child needs the love and care of their parents, as I'd been told repetitively. It was my given blessing and duty, to nurture, love, and care for this beautiful baby I'd been given. He was depending on me. Surprisingly, it was easy to smile with him and even laugh at moments. I also cried a lot. *We will get to that later.*

Chapter 6
Survival: Saved

I *t is easier said than done.*

I have seen this expression written on numerous faces as I've spoken about hardship in relationships and forgiveness before.

Quite politely, in reflection, many people would kindly explain that a step taken toward forgiveness was easier to talk about than act on. Sometimes there would be silence, raised voices, tears, or watching the person walk away.

I know that I have yelled this statement on the inside countless times when being given some piece of well-intentioned advice or feedback. It always sounds easier when it is said, but acting on it can be excruciating and laborious. With this in mind, I had to remember why I was seeking help or support. I had to remind myself that I needed help or else that I would stay prisoner to the hurt that surrounds me.

I learned during this time that I needed saving. Saving from myself, from my ex, and the negative forums of input, whether people, places or memories). Allowing someone to step into the circumstance, can be intrusive and extremely *uncomfortable*, whereas vulnerability can feel like a kick in the gut. I still painfully remember the time that I needed help and how blinded I was by my pride or shame, or both.

Doors had discreetly shut outside. It was 2 am. I had carefully told him to go to sleep. I had quietly shut the door to our bedroom. Then, I opened the front door. *Red, white and blue.* My heart skipped a beat or two and my breathing started to quicken. One officer walked towards me, while the other officer walked over to my father and checked his identity. It was all so confronting. In the early hours of the morning, in the middle of the deserted street, stood two officers and my dad. They were there for me and my son, and my husband.

Now considering what had just happened, it made sense that these people of support had arrived at my door. My dad had been on the phone with me after my intoxicated husband had rampaged through the house, inducing fear every step of the way, scaring the life out of me, before he finally left in his car. I had no idea how to move forward, I so desperately wanted my husband to be safe and not drive the car in his state. *I needed help.* So, I called the people who would lovingly help us. My parents. However, my parents in their turn called the police from fear that something might happen to *me.* I cannot imagine how they must have felt or how any rational decision was made at that moment, but they did what they thought was best. They called the police and alerted them about this horrible situation.

I was so mad that someone was trying to interfere with my life, though I had called for help in the first place. I can remember what I said, but I didn't stop to think about how I sounded.

"It's OK, everything's OK. Please leave. Leave now. Please go away. You're not needed here, not anymore. I've handled it."

I know it sounded polite, but I was not. There was an underlying tone of how *dare* you come near me and my home.

The officer gently yet firmly spoke up. He knew my name and that I had an infant inside. He knew that my husband had been drinking and was aggressive. I knew my father had intervened. I was *so* angry.

Now just before the arrival of the police and my father, I had thought things were going to settle. I had put my intoxicated husband to bed, who had bloodied his hands from smashing things around our house. He had come towards me with clenched fists and sinister intentions, but miraculously he stopped. I had told him to go to bed and sleep it off. I was calm and collected, but most likely, in shock.

The police officer spoke again, breaking the train of my thoughts of what had just happened. The other officer had subtly walked over and stood next to me. He was watching me closely, while the other spoke gently. It was then that I really, *really* listened. These two men in uniform were addressing me with authority and care. He explained how this was not the first case that they had experienced, and that it was common for them to hear about these scenarios. He said that in most cases, the offender was waiting at the door listening to everything and waiting for the opportune moment to come out and pounce. And, that the victim only hopes for the best in the present circumstance and tries to send the police away. If I would choose to stay and send them away, they could not intervene unless they were given permission.

Again, with a gentle urgency, he offered some advice. He told me to take my son and leave with my father. I could come back again to my sobered husband in the morning.

Though I had not called the police, I had called my father for help. Not because I was afraid of the violence; I was just afraid that my husband would hurt himself drunk.

My father on the other hand had other ideas of whom my husband could hurt: the woman who was trying to protect him or the infant that had no comprehension of all that what was happening. Reluctantly, my father could not keep himself from calling the police; my mother certainly urged him to do so.

Without this intervention, I honestly don't know how long I would have stayed in the abusive environment. Perhaps, I would have stayed until something so damaging occurred that couldn't be fixed. I've thought about this before, how someone could remain in such horrible circumstances of abuse. I understand to a degree why. For me, this was the love of my life, the father of my son, and the person who knew me best, who I was meant to share the rest of my life with. He would never do anything to harm me, right?

Every time I would think to go back to what was or trust my loneliness or rejection, I would remind myself of the holes in the walls. My parents encouraged me to have wisdom when approaching him moving forward, always in a public space or during the daytime before he could drink again. I did not think I would ever need anyone's help, but after this experience, I knew I had to protect Matt and myself. The help (parents, police, friends) gave me a new perspective on how we should be treated and protected. I am still shocked as I am writing this now; I cannot believe it stopped here.

Knowing now that I needed to be saved, I found that I had to stop living and re-living in horrible circumstances and overcome what was so difficult. I would say most of the time we do not have to do this alone, it is because of our pride or our shame that we try to do it alone. Yes, the hard decisions have to be made by the individual, but accepting help does not necessarily mean weakness or judgment, or more abuse. Receiving help saved my life, and that of my son, in many ways. Help provided avenues for both my son and me to have a relationship again with the other party who had been so abusive to that point. Help stopped the abuser from making poor choices that could have had even more serious consequences than the ones he has to currently live with every day.

In the past, I believed I had to serve my husband in everything that I did, and if I would make a mistake, it would be OK for him to ridicule me. I believed that submitting to my husband included being second rank to him, following his ways and speaking up only if I was being spoken to. Sometimes I was even OK coming second to other relationships. Friends had described me as a shell of the person I used to be, with no belief in myself or in what I could achieve. I needed to be saved from this dire reality as I had been stuck in it for so long. When things turned physical, I was confronted and shaken. In this vulnerable and unsafe space, I finally found the light. I was saved from further harm and was taught to stand up for myself again.

I am so grateful that my parents intervened, though I was severely mad at them for months.

They lovingly endured the worst parts of me, the hurting and healing woman who had been broken and run over. They sincerely cared for my son and me, always encouraging us to overcome the past. They tended to the basic needs and necessities of a child and financially took us in. They provided the support to work through the trauma I went through, and in turn, I could support my son fully. I do not think words or actions can ever replace the value and worth that they bestowed upon Matt and me at that time. It was a priceless moment in time of interaction of events, conversations, and actions that helped me become the woman I used to be, only now more educated and stronger.

- What is it that holds us back from accepting help?
- When can we truly admit to ourselves that we need help?
- Does it have to be when we find ourselves face down in the dirt?
- Can we listen to the people that truly care for us, who know us?
- How do we get help?

For me, it took a blue uniform and a dangerous circumstance to finally listen. Please friend, do not wait until something happens that cannot be undone. I believe I was saved that night from both my pride and my abuser. You can be saved too, however uncomfortable or scary or shameful it may be. Simply ask for help. Accept the help, please do not wait. You do not have to go about it alone.

You are not alone. It is OK to ask for help. At some point, we need to be saved *and that it is OK.*

Chapter 7
Survival: Consumed

I *remember trying to maintain my positivity* while sitting by myself in bed, in the house we had bought to raise our little boy, who was now sleeping peacefully in the room next to me. Reminiscing about that time, I can still taste the minty freshness of toothpaste in my mouth and smell the aromas of spiced meat from dinner that had been whipped up quickly after work. I can feel the softness and warmth of my bed and see the dim lighting of the lamp that used to light my bedroom.

At that moment, though I was trying my hardest to stay positive, all I could picture in my mind were various scenarios of how I could escape my everyday torture and how I could have complete silence. I did no longer want to listen to these never-ending thoughts of rejection flowing through my head like a cascading river.

Though there was no one in the house, it was still like I was battling multiple voices that had somehow claimed a right to spout their opinions over me. "You're not good enough. You're not pretty enough. You've got nothing to offer. You're hopeless and a failure. He chose someone else because he deserves better. Your life is over."

It was hard to listen to these voices and even *harder* for me not to listen to them. Hard not to feel every stab that pierced my broken and vulnerable heart, even with the pieces that were hidden away. It was hard to look in the mirror and see anything worthy of love and life. It was hard to keep going, in all honesty, and that would produce an entirely new judgemental voice of reason and self-assessment. Not only could I hear the voice of my ex with his abusive words or his sour-turned criticism, but now also my self-judgment had kicked in. Where was the light? How could I escape this consuming hell?

I made the choice. The choice to stand up to them and tell them to *shut it.*

I laughed out loud when I wrote that, "told them to shut it," but honestly, I would do just that. I probably looked like a pretty unstable person, but *every* time a negative thought came to mind, I would say: "*No,* shut it!" This went on for months: authoritatively whispering to myself at the supermarket, speaking it firmly while no one was around at work, or aggressively yelling it to myself whilst home alone. Until the voices finally began to die down, I would keep doing this. From then I started to say it internally in my mind to the voices, because I really started to believe the truth about myself and no longer their lies and rubbish.

The voices had *no right* to be in my mind. I owned this truth.

I decided to forgive myself for the mistakes I had made, and I proactively moved forward, *never pausing to revisit* the negatives that had been forgiven and dealt with. This was key to moving forward. Think of a race and how runners focus on the finish line. They do not focus on the starting point or the other runners. Although it can be beneficial to be aware of the location of others, focusing on them would lead the runner toward them, not to the endpoint. Focus on meeting the finishing line with the best foot forward, putting everything into the rhythm and strategy of winning (breathing, pace, swinging of arms and legs, eyes forward).

Now, I am not a runner, but when I did sprint as a child, I remember this is what would push me towards victory. If I saw my opponent to my left or my right and began to focus on them, I would lose motivation mentally. However, I learnt from this and I decide to turn my focus on pushing harder toward the end line. Then the opponent did not intimidate me any longer; it encouraged me to push even harder.

Coming back, it was clear that re-living past issues and pains in my mind and heart would only hold me under hurt and guilt. It would breed frustration and hate. I would become stuck in the past.

However, when I chose to let go and move forward, it was a release. I felt free of the hurt and pain, I could breathe with hope and expectation of a bright future ahead.

I became focused on learning from what I went through and living a life filled with respect and joy. I did not allow blame to come into my mind, but I allowed myself to be completely human and cry regularly. I allowed myself to grieve the loss of a relationship. I allowed time for this before telling myself to let it go and not relive it.

If I believed it and desired freedom to live in peace, I would have to start with myself and act on it. At first, I could not find these positive words to speak over myself, so I sought out help. Sometimes we don't want it but it can be a step toward freedom. For me, this help came in my father who offered it to me. He played a huge role in helping me to speak the truth over my mind. He researched and wrote down encouraging words and Bible scriptures that I could and would speak over myself daily. In the first few days, it was almost every couple of hours. When I looked in the mirror, I'd repeat these positive words over myself. "You are beautiful, there is no one like you on Earth, you are one of a kind. You are a dedicated and loving mother. You are worth it. You are loved…" I could go on.

The saying goes that out of the abundance of the heart, so the mouth speaks. I reversed that and started speaking about what I wanted to believe about myself. I began to fill my mind with positive voices and love, rather than the negative ones that had been plaguing my life. They may have been winning to begin with; they may have seemed impossible to overcome, but I can truly say that this positive reinforcement daily and sometimes hourly changed what I heard from within.

There is power in the words we speak. Both my parents taught me this and I continue to see this power in action today. We all have negative thoughts or voices that can attack us at any time. It may sound like a boss who pulls us up on the mistakes we made the week before. It may sound like a spouse who vents at us when frustrated but does not mean what they say. It may sound like a sibling or a parent or a carer or a relative of some kind that offers some advice that may not be constructive or encouraging. It may be a rebellious cry from a child who is journeying through change. The list goes on, but we are responsible for what we allow to go in and stay.

Sometimes, some things have to be stopped, even from the ones we love. If the words are tearing us apart or causing us to move towards a dark reflective place, speak about it to the source. Ask for understanding. Find a constructive and positive response rather than spiralling into a negative state of mind. If, for some reason, the person or source is unreachable, speak to a trusted and loving person about what was said or done. Speaking to someone outside of the situation can shed light and understanding which we cannot achieve alone. I would call this "accountability to wise counsel". I It could be a good friend, partner, boss or colleague, or parent. Checking our health and state of mind can only be beneficial if we are proactively seeking out healthiness in living. For me, I desired great mental health and peace, so I could continue living for my son. This developed into living for me, too.

When it comes to your mental health, what do you really desire? Chase that, however hard and long it takes; seek it out and persevere. Like a marathon, fitness cannot be achieved overnight. It takes hard work and commitment, a coach and support (perhaps even a cheer squad), a healthy diet, and rest. Perseverance and consistent training, diet, and rest: these build the fitness needed to run the lengthy marathon. In the same way, you have to work at your mental health with guidance and support, perseverance, and consistency. But rest assured, you *will* overcome the mental battle. Keep pushing through despite the pushback, lean on your support network (allow them to cheer for you and speak words that bring positivity and life), rest when you need to, and remind yourself, this negative circumstance will *not* last. *You will overcome!*

Part 2
Sealed

Chapter 8
Recovery: How Do I Focus?

*F*ind the positive element.

When Mother's Day approaches, I find myself thinking about various gifts I can give to myself. I now take joy in buying something for myself or shopping with my boy for something special, but this was not always the case. I remember that in the first year of my separation from my husband, Mother's Day was quickly approaching, and I was trying to be positive. At this stage, I was working full time, Matt was being looked after by both his grandmas on different days, and the house was being prepared for sale. To top it all off, it was report writing time, so I was bringing work home with me while testing thirty-plus students throughout the day and collating information on all of them.

Matt was growing quickly, and I knew I was missing it; this was really hurting my heart. However, I had to earn money to pay for the house and at this time I was not being supported by his dad. With the pressure of work, house payments, and lack of time with my son, I decided that it was better to sell the house.

The stress of making the house presentable and fixing it up was consuming all of my time. There were non-stop emails and calls about buyers wanting to view the house, which meant that I had to clean it all again for inspection. There were days I would have to speed home after work and clean the house that was left in a mess by the ex-husband. I would be apologising regularly because the effort the agents had to put in was not their responsibility but my ex-partner's and mine. Some days, I would go to the house in the morning to check if it was presentable before work. Those days were long and became a distant blur. The end was near and that was my focus, to sell the house. I cannot fully comprehend how I worked a new full-time job, prepared and sold a house, and continued to raise a child while maintaining my sanity. Mother's Day was not the top priority on my list, but I was still hoping for acknowledgment and love on that day and, yes sadly, from Matt's dad.

I can still remember the pink lily bouquet on the table, with a card saying: "Happy Mother's Day, love Matt." I remember the tears, the ache, the emptiness. Every other stress that had been plaguing my mind to that point instantly diminished, and I found myself looking deeply into the darkness. I knew the positive here: the thought, the purchase of flowers and a card, there was finally some acknowledgment. Yet, all I could see and feel was this deep painful emptiness. Now finally Matt's dad generously gave a gift to me, but I could only see the negative in it. My focus was solely on the lack of love and lack of his presence. I was spiralling.

This is where I learned that the power of the mind can lead to life or death.

Though I had been focusing on being positive, selling the house, working hard while pleasing my employers, and raising Matt well, one small gesture was able to tear down the positivity in my mind. My mind was honing in on an unmet expectation rather than identifying the good that had occurred, even in its smallest amount. How can we continue to allow this to happen in everyday life? If we can recognise the positive acts, circumstances, or parts of the mess, perhaps the healing process can progress into action and help further our pursuit of freedom.

As you can imagine, I was still reacting from hurt and fear. However, with this I began to understand that focusing on the unmet expectations and hurt, was progressively destroying the good around me. I decided to shift my thought processes and ask for wisdom on how to deal with my mind. I wanted to be a mentally healthy mum and woman. From then on, I would talk through all the negative thought processes with trusted mentors weekly and they would guide me to overcome the damaging lies that had crept into my mind.

To be utterly honest, this was deeply painful.

Speaking about dark thoughts and past actions, that had internally scarred my personal innocence and inner being, led me to an incredibly vulnerable place. I felt utterly exposed in bruises, hurt and shame. Was I willing to be this vulnerable to overcome a lifetime of pain? Was it worth it to uproot the dirt, or keep it buried and face the adversity when it reared its ugly head? Or try to drink or eat it away, or distract me for the rest of my life… I knew the memories would always be there unless I would work through them. This seemed like an obvious action to take, to deal with the issues quickly and completely. Like ripping a Band-Aid off quickly. Can this happen, can someone truly work through the deep hurt of the past and present, to obtain a bright future? I can honestly answer: "Yes!"

On a side note, thinking about all this I am reminded of the beauty and expense of a diamond. Thousands of people desire diamonds for their pleasure. The beauty of the stone is enough to cost thousands of dollars. Yet, it is highly unlikely that someone would stumble across a polished and perfectly cut diamond. The diamond itself in its raw form is buried deep below the Earth's crust and cannot come to the surface without the help of nature in the form of volcanic eruptions and erosion of the Earth's surface. This extraordinary stone then must go through substantial amounts of harsh treatment to finally become what it is. Diamonds are faced with extreme temperatures and pressure. They are forced through extremes, cutting and polishing away all irregularities, to create such beauty and strength in such a small stone.

I highlight this stone because the process of forming a diamond has similarities to my own journey. What was designed to break me and tear me down, only made me stronger and more beautiful! I say this to you friend, as you may be dwelling on dark thoughts of hurt and shame from past mistakes: the pressures and pain you have can be excessive but when you can work through them, you will see the reward is rewarding and priceless. Just like the diamond, you can work through the hardships of life and come out stronger, incredibly beautiful, and priceless. You are of greater worth than a diamond and you are capable of overcoming such dark places. *Don't give up!*

As for me, I met with a trusted married couple and my parents weekly to speak about the past and present any issues that were taking place. These incredible people were my first choice as they offered care, support, and unconditional love, despite my condition. Every week they would patiently sit down with me and listen to my agonising cries of pain that were painfully repetitive and hopeless. These incredible people were strong for me; they empathised with me, but they did not allow me to pause in the dark. They strenuously pulled me back to the light, deliberately showing me what purpose I had, and what compassionate love and blessings I had around me.

I candidly spoke regularly with my closest friends too. I remember a friend who would check in with me every day or two, and how she would speak sobering truth into my life that stopped my repetitive, negative talk. She said, "Beck, you acknowledged that hurt last time we spoke, and now you're ready to overcome. Remember?"

I found that the mentors, family, and friends who stepped deep into my mess, could see that going around the bush and perpetually circling my issues was not helping. I still vented about the *current* mess that occurred regularly, and they were a safe space for me to do this, but they also encouraged me to then let it go. This progressively became easier to do. Every time something happened that I did not like, I recognised for myself that it is what it is. There was nothing I could do to change that fact. However, there was one thing I could still do about it. I could release it. As long as it did not negatively affect my inner being and mental health, I would release whatever it was with these three simple words: "I forgive you." No longer would I dwell on it, it was gone. I did still vent out the frustration, but then I would let it go.

The behaviour I had witnessed from my ex-partner became the expected daily norm for him, rather than an unusual occurrence. I accepted this along with the fact that I could not change him as I recognised that I have the power to change only myself. I released my ex-partner from any of my expectations. When he could not pick Matt up for a play,

I showed understanding. When he did not communicate appropriately and put me down, I respectfully turned my ear away from those words. There were many times I had to just nod and, then, let the rubbish go. I would also keep checking in with my wise counsel in case I had been wrong or misled.

I remember one time how my ex made negative comments about how I dressed and stood. At that moment, I had to fight away tears as I went to pull Matt out of the car to leave him with his dad. Then I saw another woman's shoes on the floor; I could no longer hold myself and I wept. Matt hugged me tight, and I walked away without another word. My ex was silenced also. The next time I saw him, he tried to apologetically explain, but I said nothing about the matter in response. In fact, I passively mentioned to him that he no longer had to explain himself. I had let it go. That moment was empowering and liberating for both of us. I recognised that I would no longer expect anything from him, after all, he was not my husband anymore.

This was a release for me.

I let it go that he was with someone else and flaunted it in my face while we were supposedly working on our marriage. I let it go when he would hurl abusive and negative comments about my appearance and abilities as a woman. I let it go when he was not present or responsible for our son and his needs. I let it go every time my son was crying out for me when he would collect him for a play date or sleepover. With every negative experience with my ex-partner, I would make the choice to let it go. No expectation. Now, I can hear the common response, is that fair? He should take responsibility. He should pay for the wrongs inflicted. He should be held accountable as a father. Yet the approach to seeing any results had to be altered, as there simply was no change.

I can hear it, "There should be justice here." And *yes, there should be*. If I had fought for justice with a vengeful mindset, I might have achieved a win, but my mind and spirit would not be free. With a negative mindset, the fight was only fuelling my anger and my vengeful side, which ultimately would keep me focussed on the negative and continue to hurt *me*.

Some issues and circumstances, though, have to be dealt with properly. Abuse is unacceptable, and as such my circumstances were governed by the authorities. Matt and I were safe, and my ex was prevented from further damaging actions. Finances were also divided, and I found that fighting over money was not worth the heartache and stress. Matt's and my mental health and well-being were far more important than any extra finance. Money comes and goes, and it can always be earned again.

On the other hand, mental health can affect a person's entire life for long periods. I was very lucky to avoid medication and continued therapy. Not that they are bad in any way, I just overcame my issues without them. For me, it required continued, daily release. I do this even in the present day. The lack of interest from Matt's dad still surprises me now, but I have accepted that he does the best in his current circumstance.

What are the expectations and mindsets we have today? What are we focusing on, and is it beneficial to our mental health and well-being? Will we be a step closer to freedom by simply releasing the negative things that weigh us down? Maybe our constant focus on that bad circumstance or painful issue is not helping, but instead is tearing our internal peace away from us. Maybe you are finding that reminding yourself over and over again of the negative actions or words said, is propelling you into darkness, depression, and/or anger. Maybe the expectations we have of those that have hurt us, and continue to do so, are robbing our peace because of our lack of accepting others for who they are. Maybe the way to be free is to re-focus on the positive elements around the chaos and shift our mindset. If we start with our minds, the result can have a *far greater outcome for the future.*

Chapter 9

Recovery: Hard but Necessary—Make the Choice

*A**t some point the difficult decision* will have to be made, the inevitable choice to move forward and leave the past behind where it belongs. As I now write and think about this, my mind is drawn to the image of myself and a cliff.

I picture myself and how I am unwillingly suspended from that cliff and how I need to hold onto the edge with my bare hands, using every inch of my being to hold on to the life I lead. The daunting fear of what I will be falling into is profound, and how hard that fall would be brings more uncertainty and anxiety. What may come at the bottom is beyond terrifying! How will I be able to overcome such a traumatic and harmful drop to the ground? Will I even survive? Will I be able to function again? These thoughts and feelings plague my mind as my body in agony holds onto the cliff edge.

The overwhelming fight to hold on is torturing the mental and physical state of my being, and the attacks come from all fronts to drag me down. Gravity is doing its job. Every second, I am being drained of every ounce of strength. I feel an uncomfortable tingling in my hands as they grow sweaty and weak from holding on for so long. Every minor movement from my body and legs causes a slight shudder through my bones.

As my hands and arms struggle to pull my weight up onto the cliff surface, I realise I cannot hold on for much longer. A finger painfully slips and uncontrollably releases off the surface. The weight is unbearable and the fear increases.

At some stage, the inevitable will occur. Strength will give way. *The fall into the unknown will occur.*

The cliff symbolises past scenarios or relationships we hold onto. The fall represents letting these relationships go. It can be exhilarating to some, liberating even. To others, like me, letting go can be terrifying and painful. Either way, change is bound to occur when people are involved, we cannot control others. We are responsible for ourselves and how to resiliently and respectfully deal with circumstances that cross our path.

I had many conversations about this part of the process: letting go. I was faced with multitudes of emotions ranging from frustration, guilt and shame to pain, agony, and tears upon tears. The emotions everyone individually expressed to me, honestly and surprisingly, I felt in my heart. I understood to a degree when they were sharing their experience with me.

One lady shared about her marriage and baby boy but how her partner refused to be a part of the upbringing of her son. The rejection and desertion broke her heart. She found it incredibly difficult to find finances to support her child and her household needs. The father was trying to claim the building they were living in and even told her to move out with the baby. I remember playing with her delightfully gorgeous child and holding back tears as she busily cooked food. Her emotions were progressively becoming toxic as she lived in the pain. She could not hold back tears anymore, she could not speak out kindly, and she was about to explode.

It was in this place of tension that I asked her what she wanted. Confused, she agitatedly explained that she wanted to have a home and safe space for her child. She also mentioned that she wanted the child's father to help.

It was amazing to see that after all the hurt, she wanted the baby to have his father love him. When she realised what she wanted, she was able to release the frustrations, with raging emotions and all. I learned with this wonderful lady that finding the direction to take in the negative circumstance was vital, and then putting it into action involved hard work and determination.

Now thinking about the hurtful choices my husband was making, though completely wrong in my eyes, he was striving for what he thought was best. I was no longer what he wanted. I would not wish this upon anyone just because they did not feel like being in the relationship anymore.

Feelings come and go, but I believe relationships take commitment not just feelings. Relationships are hard work and require commitment and fierce protection. Both sides should proactively and deliberately fight for their relationship. I did fight for as long as I could, hoping for a change of mind or intentions and for a deliberate response to work at our marriage together. Unfortunately, that did not come.

It was in the depths of grief and rejection that I came to the clear understanding that I could not make him stay. No matter how much I appealed to the moral or ethical nature of his duty as a father, nothing could hold him in our marriage. I realised that I loved this man so much and that I had given my all to him. It was in love that I was going to purposefully free him from the marriage he did not want to be in any longer.

With that choice in mind, came the fears of the unknown like the cliff scenario I was talking about earlier. My son was already meeting my ex-husband's partner and they were living together. Was I going to be replaced that easily? Our house had been sold, money divided and custody orders dealt out. Was I ever going to own my own home again? Did I have to be away from my son for days at a time? Families have broken apart, as were friendships. Could I still have friendships with his family, his friends, and even his partner? Many tears were shed and the disbelief of what occurred was immense. Was I ever going to be happy again?

Letting go was daunting. Every step closer to moving forward seemingly caused multiple steps backward (or so I thought). I had to make a clear choice to move forward every time a situation presented itself. Every time, I could picture a finger being released on the cliff edge. I would neither be controlled nor try to control. It was painful, scary, and almost stupid, but the decision to let go was intentionally pushing me forward. A finger at a time, anxiety increased, but with no more fingers or strength remaining, the plunge was inevitable.

And I survived!

I think of the many people who shared their stories of their plunging from cliffs, and how they are alive to tell the tale. The emotions varied, but they all similarly made choices to move forward. It was hard for each of us but necessary for the good of everyone involved: individuals, children, friends, and extended family.

My own feelings were raw and overwhelmingly present. For this, I had to seek out the help I needed to overcome the emotional hurt and abuse; no one else could do this for me. I had to take my own productive and supportive steps to move forward, even though not everyone agreed. During this time, I found that many felt offended by me. Yet time and again, I would choose to move forward by letting go of the past.

The hard choice was to let go. It was necessary for me, for two reasons: for him and me.

Like I said before, my ex-husband did not want to be in our marriage anymore. I truly loved him, and because of this love, I could release him to his desires. I had to free him. I could not control him or manipulate him, to me that is *not love*. Again, I do not agree with the choice of leaving simply because you do not "feel it", but releasing him allowed us both to move forward.

Additionally, this choice to move forward allowed me to become my true self again without any limitation. I had to let go of the negative words and rejection. I had to let go of the neglect and the blame I held onto. I had to let go of all the memories, even those that brought complete joy and happiness, the days that led me to fall in love, and release them to the past.

I also had to let go of the relationships that were breathing negativity between us both. It was hard, but hold on I will self-correct, and it was excruciating; only when this happened completely, I found peace. It was really difficult to put into motion, but it helped me move forward on my journey to love and trust again. I even found a place of love and *respect for my ex-husband and his partner.*

Chapter 10

Recovery: Letting Go

S *o, what do I mean by letting go?*

Are we letting the parties involved go free without judgment, punishment, or retribution?

Are we turning a blind eye to what happened and carefully bottling the hurt inside?

Are we putting up walls around our hearts, so that the pain never penetrates our hearts again?

Are we forgetting whatever happened and choosing to think or dream up something that contrasts to replace the horrible memories?

No.

Letting go is another part of the forgiving process. Eventually, at some point in life's journey, we should come to a place of readiness to move forward, to let go. After the choice to forgive. After the daily action of reminding ourselves, we have chosen to forgive, every time. After, and occasionally still during, venting out the frustration of hurt.

We will find it is time to move forward. *That requires letting go of what has been done.*

Just like choosing to forgive, we need to choose to let go.

When I was newly married, I was far from being the best cook. I understood the basics, I could follow recipes, and sometimes, I would reach out of my comfort zone and try something new.

However, it felt like every time I cooked it was not good enough for my husband. A little encouragement and guidance would have been helpful, as I can readily admit that I am still a learner in the kitchen, and perhaps I will hold that perspective of myself for the future. No, he made some hurtful probing comments about how I could improve my cooking, but instead of saying something, I bottled the feelings in. After a few failed attempts, my view of cooking became quite negative. In fact, I started to loathe cooking. More often, I would repeat the recipes that worked and were appreciated, but I did not dare venture into something new. Following instructions, I would create a minimal, acceptable meal, and be completely miserable in the act! It became one of my most hated chores to complete. I even preferred to clean the bathrooms!

Years later, I found that despite the choices I had made to forgive and move forward, I still held a negative mindset about cooking. Family and friends would praise me for my cooking but for some reason, I was stuck in that bad space. My son would eat every one of my meals, and he would mostly polish the plate. However, instead of thinking I was a good cook, I told myself that it was my directed discipline in his eating. I told myself that these people encouraged me because of the depressive state I was in and that it had nothing to do with my skills.

At the time of my marriage, my husband wanted to improve my abilities in the kitchen. However, I had taken something he said to improve in a negative way and let this negative perception repeat itself in my mind every time I cooked. It was horrible. It festered into something bigger than it was. As I washed and cut vegetables, I would picture the conversation, my every failed attempt at food, and even see a look of disgust or held-back laughter at the taste of any meal I provided. Though he could have handled it better, he is still human and so am I. I just know that this memory of cooking still impacted my life years after the comment was first made. As a result, it halted my progress in this area of cooking.

Why would I want to stay in such a place of negativity?

This example of holding onto the negative held me back from finding happiness in the kitchen. I could not find any joy in providing and cooking for anyone, not my son, my family nor even my friends. I could not embrace a hobby that could be fun.

This also applies to other examples such as intimacy, friendships, hobbies, travel, you name it. Not letting go stops you from moving forward with any of these. It creates an avoidance of that area of life. It brings darkness around circumstances that you are supposed to enjoy and bravely attempt. It can stop us from venturing into the unknown. It can rob us of future endeavours and adventures, locking us into a lonely and damaged place.

Nevertheless, using this example of cooking in my world, there are ways to let go and move forward, to escape the darkness. For me, people were gracious around me, my parents understood me, *for a time*. They allowed me to avoid cooking for a while, or only cook the basics. They encouraged me when I was branching out a little in the kitchen, and I can see now that they were being strategic with that. Luckily, my son always ate my food, so it was easy to cook for him, but for others I would always find ways to avoid the chore. It was difficult for me to even think about making a meal, but I knew that I could not live like this forever. I loved my family and friends, and I knew that for me, providing a meal for them is another way that I could show love. I realised that one negative memory I was holding onto was now stopping me from my love towards others. My unforgiveness towards myself was ultimately holding my happiness back. I was being robbed of my own freedom and joy, and *I was the culprit*.

Becoming aware of the holding on, was my first step forward to letting go.

No one could release me from what had happened in my world but me. I had to choose to let go. After choosing to forgive, acting on that choice every day and speaking with support regularly, to know that I was moving in the healthiest and most beneficial direction, were vital. I found that after those steps, it was time to let it go. I was no longer in a space that was detrimental to my well-being and safety. I was in a healthier state of mind and ready to face the attacks that were a part of my everyday life. I was no longer going to live under the negative memories plaguing my mind and feelings. I no longer wanted to tightly grip the lies and depression that came with the memories. I found that when I began to lift my fingers from the hurtful past, I could see the truth and the freedom it held.

I recognised that holding on was not saving my life, but that it was destroying it. I realised that holding on did not help me receive retribution or justice; it only brought confusion and aggravation. So much negativity was birthed from holding onto damaging past occurrences. It was my responsibility to see that I was the one holding on. My support network may have subtly highlighted how I was holding on to negative moments, but I had to see for myself what I was in fact doing. Revisiting these memories only held me in the past. I could not move forward without releasing my grip. And when I finally became aware, I could act on the process of letting go.

Letting go can help you see the truth.

The truth is: I *can* cook, and I can cook *well*. The meals were always edible and sometimes they were really tasty. Gosh, I am smiling while writing this. In my marriage, I cooked all the time despite the regular criticism. Every meal brought improvement, quicker preparation time and productivity. I made better taste and portion judgments. Meals were made for the baby and grown-ups in our home after I had been working a full day while nurturing and playing with a toddler. He was fed while things were being prepared, washed, and served. Although I heard constant criticism, I have to say that there was never any food left over. The food disappeared sometimes before I had even eaten for myself. Looking back, I now realise that as a matter of fact my cooking was good; it was just the criticism that I was holding on to that coloured my perception. Without choosing to let go of the horrible memories, I would not be able to share with you the positives of that time. I would be stuck in the darkness of lies and confusion.

I believe that holding on to unforgiveness produces a festering place of negativity that opens up even more pain and suffering. It is no longer that one moment of pain-causing damage, but it births lies and confusion from the place of unforgiveness that manipulates and destroys anything in its path. Current and future relationships are affected by this inner torment that we create when we hold onto past hurts.

I think that sometimes we cling to burdens that we are never meant to carry. We hold on, perhaps because it is too painful to face. Perhaps we think we need to face it alone. Maybe there is shame, guilt, or anger.

However, *Friend, we were designed to live free. We have a free will and a free choice.*

With unforgiveness, we hold onto things that degrade our identities and self-worth. Why would we choose to hold onto something that only hurts us further? With this small but significant example of cooking in my life, I found my self-worth was severely lacking. I found that I alone was degrading myself. By repeating the negative words and holding onto the memories that tore me down, I was breaking myself over and over again. I was actively choosing to hold on to the negative. I could no longer blame the negative words spoken; I was the one responsible for holding on.

Culturally, I was brought up to be the cook of the home, a great homemaker who knows how to cook. I was being robbed of this because I was holding onto the unforgiveness from years back. Whether it had been intentional or unintentional hurt, holding on to it only caused further damage.

Maybe there is something you are holding onto. Something that affects your lifestyle because of a specific word said, or action done in the past. Yes, it may be unjust and unfair. But I urge you, why hold onto it and hurt yourself any further?

Friend, let it go.

Additionally, *if there are constant offensive circumstances, letting go can still be achieved.*

Every person's situation is different, but the beneficial process of letting go can still happen even when there is current, re-occurring hurt. The pivotal focus here is not on the negative circumstances but on how to process them. Just like choosing to forgive, choosing to release the frustrations, memories and hurt, helps to let go. The weight of holding onto the negative will be lifted each time you let go.

This practice becomes an everyday lifestyle, like brushing our teeth. Every time I prepare a meal, I let go of the memories that once plagued my mind and start afresh. I tell them no, and I stop the thoughts. I remind myself that I can cook and well.

Hopefully, you are not in a circumstance where there is repetitive abuse, but if so, please remember that you do not have to face any of it alone. Seeking healthy and constructive support around you helps you to process the hurt healthily and safely. You can reach out to support networks through community health organisations, professional services through your doctor, or counselling networks through various sources.

Never forget, you are not alone. There are support services that can journey with you, just ask for help. It is OK.

What I learned here was that in life we will certainly experience pain, but it is how we overcome it that really matters. Not living in the hurt but rather taking the good, like growth, perseverance and resilience, and releasing the bad, like negativity, shame, guilt, depression and anxiety. Facing hurt every day can be tiring and degrading but forgiving and letting go strengthen us to move forward.

This process enables and empowers us to overcome the damage every time. Just imagine doing that daily. How our inner strength will develop if we truly understand how to process and let go.

I do not take away from how hard this is. Still now, as I cook something, the thoughts try to creep back and break my progress of moving forward. But I stop them. I do not relive the memories. After constructively processing those moments of hurt, I actively choose to let go and to continue to let go.

Friend, letting go of the things that caused me so much suffering allowed me to step back into a free and happy lifestyle. I was free to find myself again. I became an even better 'me' than before I was married and before any abuse had occurred in my world. Understanding how the process worked liberated me and helped me to act on it. Now I can let go every time; sometimes with a little delay, but eventually every time.

Letting go involves the choice to do so, understanding that we are free and can live our lives liberated from unforgiveness. There is so much truth that we fail to see whilst holding onto the negative past, creating for ourselves a dark and detrimental space of a mentality that can only destroy. In this process, we never have to go it alone, and the thought to do so in itself is a lie. No pride, shame, or guilt demands us to live life alone or go about life alone, we can reach out for help, always.

I hope you understand that letting go will liberate you, empower you, and ultimately strengthen you. It allows life to move forward with positivity and happiness. It allows you to face hurtful situations healthily and beneficially. You can overcome. You *will* overcome. *You've got this.*

Chapter 11

Recovery: Time to Accept Change

I really wanted my marriage to work out. How many times have I tried to work out the differences between my husband and me and make our marriage work?

I remember pleading with him to come back, to work things out, to see that I had changed, to try again. I tried to show him the differences in our home or finances or anything else that he used to complained about. I reminded him of our commitment to each other, of our vows, to remember the man who he said he was. I pleaded with the moral and ethical man that he presented himself to be. I cried out to God in my prayers for answers, for suggestions, for some kind of gift that could bring us back together.

The truth is…I was willing to do anything. I was willing to give up everything just to avoid separation and divorce. I had given my all to this man and was willing to give up all for this relationship. But I could not speak to just anyone about my hopeful inclinations toward my marriage, as most people were too protective and angry at my husband, to allow such thoughts to continue.

However, as time is told to heal all wounds, I eventually found my emotions coming into balance. I found resolve and reason during our separation. It was not in the past, of what had been, that I found this resolve but rather in the present. Though there had been so many positive memories and so many good choices had been made, that was no longer my current situation.

With every encounter, every word spoken, and every action taken, I saw an increase in his spite, anger and hate. This was not always directed at me, but I was usually on the receiving end. I recognised that there was a good reason for everyone in my life to be protecting me. I would not be safe with this man. I recognised that even though I had been in love and made a commitment in front of everyone I knew, the man I had chosen was now actively and consciously walking away from me. He had chosen another over me and broken our commitment. The vows we had made were pointless to him and now, I was merely an inconvenience holding him back.

I was stopping this man's freedom.

***

It was about six to seven months into our separation, and we were invited to a birthday on a night-time cruise. It was one of those party cruises with nibbles and entertainment. When I received the invite, I almost responded straightaway with a "no", as things were so uncertain with Matt and his dad. Unfortunately, I had taken to not seeing anyone, reserving my outings to specific people who were aware of our situation. Surprisingly, my desire to go to this party was larger than I expected. I loved the person we were going to celebrate and most of my family were attending, many coming from inter-state. If I did not go, it would be just me at home, as Matt would most likely go to his dad's for the night.

The thought of asking to take Matt for a night that belonged to his dad scared me. I had asked for extra days in the few months after our separation, but I felt embarrassed at the rejection each time and broken from my loss of love.

Despite these feelings, life went on and people included me in their celebrations. We had weddings, parties, and family gatherings almost fortnightly. It was difficult to attend joyful events when people were expecting the entire family to attend. Most of my family waited to cuddle Matt and play with him, but it was difficult for me to speak about where his dad was.

His dad would be quite harsh with me when I asked for additional days, calling me selfish or uncaring towards their father-son relationship. I would feel incredibly guilty, thinking I was at fault for making such a request. The discussions turned so negatively that I would find myself all over the place with my emotions. My family would encourage me to speak as little as possible to him, to avoid the after-effects that they witnessed. It must have been so hard for them to just watch and not be able to do anything.

After multiple instances, I chose to forfeit events if I could not have Matt present. Looking back now, I think I did this because I was ashamed of being alone. I was hoping for things to be resolved before the public knew of our breakup. I wanted to avoid conversations about what was going on.

The few talks I allowed ended in tears and shame on my part and of course, awkwardness. I over-thought conversations and ideas, pushing my emotions to various extremes. It would tire my body out so that I could not function afterward.

I think of that emoji with the worried look on the face and the open, scattered brain… If I could draw a picture of what was happening to me, it would look like that. Yes, it was as dramatic as it sounds or looks, if you know the emoji. I cringe at the inner reaction that would take place when needed to converse with my ex-husband, back in those days. The amount of anxiety and brokenness caused so much damage to me.

Matt's dad allowed him to come to the party with me. What a relief it was!

I tell you, when the Bible says, "Ask and you will receive," I have to fully agree with it. It was difficult to step up and accept this new normal that our lives had become. Matt was a part of both families and worlds, he should have been seeing both sides and building relationships all around. Court orders cannot control event dates and family gatherings. They cannot build a relationship. I realised that one day, Matt's dad and I would have to learn to compromise and respect one another enough to allow Matt to be free with our families. Both of us are still working on this respect for the sake of our child, but the progression has been aided by forgiveness and deliberate action to show respect.

I tell you this story and learning point because these circumstances of control were a regular negative occurrence for me during that year. The weekly occurrence built up stress and anxiety every time that I would communicate with Matt's dad and caused further damage to my mind and body. That year of stress was enough to destroy me if I did not have my own village to save and build me every time. It caused ridiculous weight loss, sleep deprivation and isolation. The amount of hardship was incredible. The more I held onto the man who desired freedom, the more I deteriorated. I am not the type to scream and yell… Oh, but how I wanted to! Internalising everything was killing me quietly and quickly. I had chosen to forgive and let go, now it was time to accept the change in our circumstances.

It truly was *my* fault that I was in this negative space, holding on to whatever was lingering between my husband and me. This is clear to me now. With hindsight, I know now that I was holding onto the past, thinking there was a future. I was fighting for something that the other person did not want. I was judging myself, placing unreasonable expectations on him, and hoping for a resolution. I was actively communicating through a closed and sealed-off door.

After this epiphany, I remember the next step I acted on. I had to be completely sure that there was no chance for our relationship to continue. It was going to be an incredibly hard conversation, but I needed to know. We were meeting outside my parent's house, and I began to carefully pick Matt up out of the car seat. I turned to my husband at the time and asked, "Do you want this marriage? Do you want us?"

He nonchalantly looked me in the eyes and said, "No. I've closed this chapter of my life."

I then hugged Matt closer, feeling my heartbreak again. I could not help the tears flowing from my eyes. I mumbled a "thank you for honesty" and walked away. He quickly jumped in his car and drove away.

I had learned a valuable lesson that day. It was time to accept what was going on, it was time to accept the choice that the person I loved most was making. If I truly loved him, I would release him and not try to control him. In doing this, I also would be free from this relationship. It was the choice we were both making. With this came changes in all areas of our relationship. Mutual respect and understanding we had to work at, daily. We no longer could abide by normal family rules, if there is such a thing. We had to be flexible and remain open to communication.

However, the communication had to be constructive, healthy and focused. We no longer spoke about ourselves but focused on Matt. He was the central focal point for any communication.

Interestingly, when I finally made this choice in my heart, the outworking of it became increasingly easy to follow through with. We had already set court orders and financial separation in place. The paperwork came through a couple of months after the sale of the house. The discussion around selling the house was always negative on his part, as he thought we would keep the house together as an asset. Several times, I would hear the words "I can't believe she sold the house" from outside sources who were still communicating with him.

There were many compromises made while we were married and working together, but that had now changed. We were separated, working towards divorce, and with that change came blessings and consequences. We both had to learn how to have shared relationships and responsibilities without having a personal relationship that connected the two of us.

The challenges seemed to pop up continually.

I soon learned that finances were a difficult topic to discuss and resolve. Already there was a lack of trust and direction with finances when we were married, so now that we were separated, I had to apply healthy strict boundaries. I had to make sure that he would not know anything about my finances or what I dreamed to do. To be honest, this was so hard as to me he had been my best friend; I would tell him everything. But now..., now I could tell him *nothing*.

He knew me, though. He knew how to ask and how to tease information out of me, and he tried. So, it was really important for me to stick to the boundaries, or I only had myself to blame for further discomfort between us.

Many people would ask me questions about child support and what he was contributing to raising Matt. Yet, I could not approach him about any of this; it was not only difficult but almost useless. By law, I should have received regular payments from him, but I found that demanding and taking money from him, even for this purpose, made the fragile relationship between Matt, him and me toxic. I had to make a hard decision regarding all this. It was a choice I desperately prayed into and eventually found my resolve. What was really more important? Amongst all this, what was really at stake? If Matt could have a positive relationship with his dad in the future, then why not fight for that? If that meant, that I had to surrender my right to financial support for the sake of my son, then so be it.

It did require loads of patience and a financial sacrifice on my part, but in the long run, it would benefit Matt and his dad, and therefore me. The choice to not pursue child support was something we could manage. I had some savings and a home to live in without cost, for which I will forever be grateful to my parents. When possible, I would work and save as much as possible, budgeting and spending only on necessities.

With this, I also learned to trust both sets of grandparents for the safety of my son as I had to ask for their help in looking after him. I always desired to be a "stay-at-home mum", but we needed finances if we wanted to survive. In the end, this proved to be quite positive in my relationship with my in-laws as they would encourage me to visit Matt whenever he was with them and have dinner with him weekly.

Sometimes Matt would stay with his grandparents and at others with his dad at his apartment. On the days that he went to his dad's, Matt was very emotional and expressed through words and tears that he wanted his *mumma*. So, I would go to the grandparents after work and play with him. If I was not working, I would take him out for the day. It was interesting, abiding by the law in this way.

Even though court orders were in place for shared custody, his dad's side of the family included me wherever possible, and I would go see Matt to help Matt. In fact, my in-laws did not agree with the cold letter of the court orders; they believed that a child should not at all be separated from their mother. As time progressed, it became so clear to me that at any rate relationships are of greater value than finances.

For this reason, I chose to remove the financial hurdle from the relationship. Now I am not saying that this necessarily was right. Do I think both parents should support their children? Absolutely. I just believe that while accepting change, we should apply grace. Was I able to work and provide for Matt? Yes. Was sacrifice needed? Definitely. Finances were a hurdle to developing a positive relationship for us to work things out for the sake of our son. Here, I was able to compromise on finances for a little while to gain a positive relationship.

Additionally, to build respect in a relationship I found that it had to be modelled and applied regardless of the return. Although I was working on call, I had to be organised in case Matt's dad did not pick him up. This was a regular occurrence without warning or communication. Pick up time would be approaching for Matt's dad but there was no call or message. Matt would ask, "Am I staying home mummy?" Every time he asked this, I would think I was happy but honestly, I was also sad. Sad that the priorities and relationships we fight for differ from person to person. I cannot comprehend how different Matt's dad and I were on this matter of priorities, but, again, I would choose to accept the change occurring every day between us.

I hoped to communicate with Matt's dad many times, that Matt had the love language of time and needed that from us both, but I had to wait for the correct timing. The lack of his dad's presence was noticeable. It became the topic of discussion with family and friends around us.

The talk revolved around the lack of responsibility and respect for me, and this would be highlighted regularly. Again, this was coming from people who loved us, but I could not change this man. He made his choices and I had to respect them. I would not allow Matt to be caught in the middle. I stepped up to the receiving end. Regardless of everything, Matt would always be looked after, his health protected and nurtured. Matt would not lack in anything, except maybe in having a present father. The early days were hard, but many beautifully loving men filled the role, like both his grandpas and his uncles.

It came down to the question, "What are the blessing and benefits here?"

I could step up as the authority in Matt's life. I could take ownership and responsibility for what would happen moving forward. Though I desired partnership and joint decision-making, it was left up to me to follow through with parenthood.

The lack of respect was hurtful and belittling, but I chose to build my view of myself. I could envision the woman I was and who I wanted to be. I worked hard to be healthy, positive and grounded in who I was, to give Matt a healthy parent. I found respect for myself. This understanding of myself stopped the disrespect from others from affecting me. My value did not come from or depend on anyone else but God and me.

The lack of responsibility was not for me to follow up on or stress over. This was not my problem; this grown man was not my responsibility. Instead of blaming myself, I recognised this was another aspect I had to release about my ex-husband. His actions do not reflect on Matt. They may affect us, but I could have control over how much it did. Matt would have to work through the emotional effects when he was mature enough but if I could, I wanted to help us both deal with this as healthily and respectfully as possible. I spoke to counsellors about what preventative actions could be taken. I read books and listened to various sources of wisdom. With all this knowledge, I found that one of the best ways forward for Matt and I was forgiveness.

As the lack of partnership became more and more noticeable to all around us, so too grew the need to forgive, and to keep forgiving. People would share their opinions on these circumstances and tear away any positivity from my mind. I would have to continually rebuild positive mindsets and choose again to forgive, teaching this to anyone as they conversed with me. I think that even at his young age Matt witnessed many moments of this cycle, and, to my surprise, he would do the same and choose to forgive his dad.

You see, all of this had become my new norm in life. Even though I had been victimised in many ways, I could choose to stay focussed on being the victim and live in fear, hurt, rejection, pity, shame. The list could go on. As such, I could choose to be the victim, to live solely from a victim mindset. But what life would that be? How could anyone live like that for prolonged amounts of time? I could not. I would not! We completely needed to accept our changed lifestyle to achieve freedom. Matt and I were going to be free. Our journey would be filled with happiness, healthiness, and passion for living. No more holding back. The choice was *to live life to its fullest.*

Chapter 12
Recovery: Support

When certain bones are broken in the body, the body tends to initiate the healing process for the bone. It is pretty incredible how the human body works to restore what was not functioning as it once was.

Sometimes, the broken or fractured bone can heal incorrectly as it forms anew. This happens quickly as the body is trying to mend itself. If the bone heals in the incorrect position, this can lead to further suffering and damage.

When it heals incorrectly, the doctor will again have to break the incorrectly healed bone, out of that wrong position, and reset it in the correct direction. Screws and/or metal plates are inserted to hold the bones in place to encourage correct healing. A cast will safely cover the recovering injury and the person cannot use the broken area until a full recovery, which could involve weeks, or perhaps months. This is important so that the affected body part can be fully used for the rest of life without any weakness or disability or discomforts to other areas of the body. The right healing process, though uncomfortable, long and costly, always provides greater reward than the quick fix.

This picture of healing a broken bone crossed my mind during a discussion I had about forgiveness, and it just made sense. Most of the time, people in society want things to happen quickly. Love, finances, education, fun times, bad times, exam periods, medical procedures, relationships, we want them almost instantly, or to be finished just as quickly. We want positive things quickly, like graduating, or buying a car or house, or falling in love. We want it to happen now. We want to immediately experience all the positive feelings and emotions that follow such events or happenings. On the other hand, we want the negative things that occur, such as medical procedures, stressful work or study periods, broken relationships etc. to end quickly. We do not like to dwell in hardship for long periods, let alone desire it; we do not want to suffer the hurt or discomfort.

Sometimes a quick fix could actually lead to more damage or suffering in other areas of the body. Sometimes, the bone has to be re-broken and foreign metals have to be put in place to hold the bone together. It takes time and commitment to heal physically and well. It takes time and commitment to heal mentally and emotionally well, too.

I believe a relationship breakdown can be treated similarly. If we have our heart broken or hurt, our mind switches on to process all the negative and hurtful words or actions that have happened around the time of hurt. It tries to process thoughts and events that have taken place, find cause and resolution, find the "why" or the "how". It can be very painful to revisit everything as the mind travels through the history of that relationship and sometimes it can be too painful. Often at those times, we tend to apply *the quick fix to stop the pain*. We can try to distract the mind with another more pleasing idea or notion. We may replace the pain with a block or wall so that the mind cannot go back there. We might even drown out any thoughts leading our mind to the source of pain. Over time this may seem like healing, but in reality we have made the healing process harder.

I have revisited many moments of the time when I was hurt by my ex-husband, not just the present circumstances that were taking place. It always surprises me to me that I would become angry all over again for things that had happened to me years ago, and that I thought that I had dealt with. My mind was unnecessarily urging me to get even more angry, hurt and depressed. It was horrible.

I wonder if that has happened to you? Can you identify a moment in time when it was too difficult to revisit and face the hurt incurred?

Thinking about the healing process of the bone, a quick unguided healing technique could lead to further damage, right? In the same way, unguided healing and overcoming of such trauma, mental and emotional hurt could lead to further damage of relationships in the future.

What am I trying to say here? I believe we need help; we need support, we need a "village" to live amongst and learn from, and sometimes by which to be looked after. We need another trusted voice of reason to support our healing journey, whether from a professional, or a best friend, a relative or a neighbour.

I had trusted and loving family friends who had wisdom and insight, and who journeyed with me in love and patience. I had my parents who walked by my side through the darkest days, gently encouraging me when I was a disgusting rude mess. I will be forever grateful for them. I had specific friends who had differing views on my approach, but their love never faltered for me. I had family members who just hugged and held me, cried with me, listened and prayed. I had others sending words of encouragement and grace.

The "village" of people around me was my support, my backbone, and my pick-me-up when I could not do that for myself. Because of this support network, I was able to find a healthy outlook on life. I was able to stand again, walk again, and, finally, love again.

It may be hard for you to trust people or professionals. But I would not have made it through on my own. The advice from the "village" helping me supported my healing journey and stopped any unhealthy formations or beliefs from occurring. They witnessed the lies I spoke over myself and stopped them from becoming core beliefs. Although, I did not listen to everything that they said as not everything was relevant, I most certainly benefitted from the support around me.

Like the body finding the best course to healing so that its parts can fully function, support networks are a part of the healing journey of forgiveness. Support networks should be positive, caring, and loving. They should also be honest, patient, and empowering. They are human and people will make mistakes. Just remember the motivation behind any support is to see you restored to your true self without anything holding you back. If your trauma or hurt is holding you back from having healthy relationships, your support network should partner with you to empower you to learn to trust again, while also gaining wisdom from *the circumstance you experienced.*

Chapter 13
Back to School, on Another Tangent...

R^{epeat, repeat, and repeat.}

    1 x 1 = 1
    1 x 2 = 2
    1 x 3 = 3

Do you know how you become proficient in mathematics? You practice and repeat the idea over and over again.

At school, we were encouraged to constantly memorise and apply repetition to study and become proficient in the concept taught. This we then had to apply in a test, exam or assignment to gain the reward of retained knowledge and acknowledged success. This strategy of repetition helps us to soak up knowledge that we can outwork in our life.

Although this seems straightforward, it is not always enjoyable. The repetitive work can be boring at times, frustratingly difficult, and sporadically confusing. Without someone to cheer for me or steer me in the right direction, I would have given up.

Teachers repeat the same strategy with their students for days or weeks, in order for the student's brain to embrace the principles and retain the information they need to know. Every day they use the same language and provide regular practice so that students can gain the knowledge they need to solve future problems. After days, maybe weeks of repetition, students eventually grasp and understand how to apply the concept that is being taught. It is remarkable how beneficial repetition is when it is used correctly.

What are we repeating in our minds right now? What are we reliving over and over to affect our mindset and confidence?

It is said that if you want to replace a habit, you have to repetitively replace the bad habit with a good one over a period of time. Then, before you know it, you will be free of that bad habit. The negative habit is eventually less likely to be used or acted on, because the person is proactively working on something more beneficial and positive to their well-being.

Repetition was a huge part of my forgiveness journey. Every day, every minute, every second, as negative thoughts would drift across my mind, I would choose to forgive. This became my strategy to overcome hurt, grief and anger. I did not block it out or replace it with a distraction. I faced it with forgiveness.

Let's rewind a little.

Early in the process, after our separation, we mutually agreed upon financial separation and custody orders. This was done quickly to stop the financial manipulation that was occurring. It was so difficult working through these proceedings and trying to be amicable. I remember the private cries for help as I began to understand the difficult fact that legally I would not be able to see my son every day. Although this was the law, my heart ached for justice. Still to this day, that does not sit right with me.

I began to embrace hopelessness as, completely heart broken, I worked my way through the stone-cold legal documents with my solicitor. The solicitor, my parents and my trusted friends could see that I was becoming more depressed with how the legalities were being set out. These incredible people gently pointed out that I needed to persevere through the hard times. My son loved me and needed me. There were multiple discussions around the future and how there was a light at the end of the tunnel. I made a choice one dark day when I could think nothing more but selfish, negative thoughts. I chose in that desperate hour despite all the darkness that I would believe again, I would again hope for justice.

This initiated a repetitive cycle of thinking in my mind. This time, it was going to be a cycle of positive repetition. This cycle of positive repetition had to replace the negative thoughts that were flooding my mind.

I was financing a house that I was not living in and ensuring my child's well-being all on my own, although we agreed to have a life and child together. I was agreeably yet painfully paying debts I had not known we had. With all the verbal abuse and negativity filling the airways to my mind, I found it easier to just pay what was brought forward to me. It was hard to be under financial strain with someone who was not honest or trustworthy. The amount of stress that had pulverised my peace *all because of money,* I can tell you it was insane! When I read about the power of money and how it affects people, I used to think the writer was just exaggerating. However, I truly experienced the negative effect money can have on people and it radically changed how I approached every circumstance moving forward.

I needed to be free from any financial control. I did not need or want to finance a lifestyle that went against my own beliefs, morals and ethics. I did not want to fulfil responsibilities that were not mine at all, or that were not related to the care for my son. With the remaining strength I had left during that exhausting period, I acted on the repetition in my mind. I chose to put one foot in front of the other and take the next step toward the goal: my freedom.

> *The first step,* set up financial separation and custody orders.
> *The second step,* break financial ties with the person I had no trust in.
> *The third step,* sell the house.

Every time I found doubt or fear creeping in, I repeated to myself what was to come. Freedom from control. Freedom from stress. Freedom financially. Repetition urged me to push forward, to value myself enough to be free. If I had not focused on the repetition of one foot in front of the other and the constant reminders of freedom to come, I would have been stuck between two minds of fear and doubt. Repetition helped me to take action and move forward.

Surprisingly, this was easier to do than I thought. Within six months our house sold, the legal separation was approved, and I was finally totally free of this man's control. I kept repeating to myself, one step at a time, a day at a time... and we got there! It was daunting. Sometimes I felt like I was walking on thin ice. Every act of kindness on my part, every time I stopped a response that would only fuel the fire, every time I chose to let it go, my ex could only see an example of amicability. When he had his moments of calm, I could share with him the importance of working together for Matt. Eventually we both could amicably agree, and we made it through the legalities.

I want to encourage you with this. Take a step at a time, no matter how hard things get. You will move forward if you just take a step forward, however fast or slow you go. Look up now and then toward the end goal and know in your heart where you want to go. Repeat to yourself, take the next step, you can do it. Take it, *you can do it!*

Sometimes life experiences really suck, they are just horrible. It can be hard to process anything or even see where we are going to tread next. I would like to remind you of that moment I felt hopeless and when I increasingly delved into the dark thoughts about life. Thanks to the consistent support network around me, I remembered why I am here and who I live for. The repetitive words that flowed through my mind, convinced me of how much Matt's love encapsulates my world. At some point, I had to choose whether to listen or fade away for good.

Our hearts and minds process uniquely and that is OK.

It can be difficult for others to understand what is happening to you. They can empathise with you and love you throughout your hardship. There will be genuine and caring people who want to pull you out of hopelessness and depression so that you can achieve your dreams and overcome hardship. It is difficult to listen, but remember the goal is to be free of these hardships and live your life to the fullest. If pain, hurt, trauma is holding you back, allow some support to guide you back to freedom, *the freedom to be you again.*

Chapter 14
Moving Forward: Overcoming the Control

*W*hen we love someone, there is a deep desire to please and honour them. Children desire to please their parents, followers their leaders, congregations their pastors, husbands their wives, and *vice versa*. Human nature leans towards the need to serve and give openly to the love of their lives, without expectation of return. The phrase "Give and you will receive" comes to mind. I am reminded of how many beautiful examples of love exist in the world and how they require giving.

I remember sitting at a friend's house with her baby. We were chatting about the life and struggles of being young mums. The responsibility of raising a child while maintaining yourself was a popular topic. Her baby was entertaining himself on the floor but I could not help but play with him.

Her phone buzzed and she apologised for it. I encouraged her to answer, ensuring her I will be OK, after all I had the baby. She said she could call back later as it was just her husband, but I insisted that she'd answer. It was her husband checking in to see how her day was going. Yes, he had given her a kiss goodbye in the morning, yet he was still looking out for her, sometimes calling twice or three times. He was at work yet thinking of her and her child; this was something that warmed my heart. I loved this example of unconditional love.

Thinking of unconditional love, I also think of the mother who keeps the house immaculately clean and strategically prepares multiple meals for the family. I think of the little boy who picks flowers for his mother and grandmother without any purpose other than to make them smile. The grandfather who irrevocably gives in to every request of his grandchild, even when the parents plead with him to stop. Love can be a beautiful drive to give.

Occasionally, the aspirations to please and be loved are not reciprocated. This does not always halt the desire to please; in fact, it can increase it. Due to this desire to love and please, there was an increase in acts of service to encourage affection toward the other. At times, relationships formed that were not healthy or were unwanted.

Thinking of relationships, I know I befriended many people without a second thought even though they did not always turn out to be the right friends. My parents guided me through relationships, explaining how friends give and receive, how there are seasons of taking and seasons of receiving but never of just always taking.

Still, I was one of these people who wanted to be loved and accepted. I realised that in my need to please and love and be loved, I found myself eventually in a friendship marked by negative behaviour.

At school, there was bullying, manipulation and control that subtly surrounded me. I suffered some negative experiences as I wanted to make my friends happy. My best friend in high school was completely different to me, just like opposites attract. She was from another culture and upbringing, she had different beliefs and she had more freedom than I had ever encountered as an adolescent. We connected as friends straight away. She was strong, smart, and outgoing. She was friendly and funny. She was adventurous and spontaneous. I loved the crazy situations we often got ourselves into.

At the time, I had no idea that this friend exerted control over me. I thought it was normal to be told what to do and how to do it. But then she started hitting me. The first time she slapped me was because I did not listen to her, and I thought I had done something wrong and deserved the punishment. As these interactions occurred, the focus was never on her actions but always on mine. I hoped our friendship and my resolve to improve my behaviour would overcome the negative circumstances unfolding weekly, but this negative and unacceptable behaviour did not stop. The negative words and random hits or nudges when I would not listen grew worse as we grew older. After a few years of this, I began to learn that I should not put up with violence of any kind. I cannot fathom how long I stayed in this space of friendship, or even why I did, as it was obvious that I was being treated badly.

We had started out so well, there were fun-loving moments and unique experiences. Somehow though, her need for control began to grow, increasing as we developed into young women. This friendship had lasted three years but towards the end it was being held by threads. I started to regularly avoid her during lunchtimes. Though I could barely say she was my friend, everyone at school was under the impression we were best friends.

One day, on the way back from a field trip, she was pinching, hitting and speaking nasty comments in my ear. I thought that

Chapter 14

I could ignore her for a little, but she slapped my arm again hard because I was not responding. I glared at her, and she would ask the question again, but I could not speak. I rubbed my arm as it was stinging and tried to hold back the tears. In those moments, it was hard to articulate anything when I felt pain, pain from both the physical hurt and the pain in my heart. She was supposed to be my best friend how could this behaviour be OK? How could anyone just watch and allow it? She slapped the same place again, but this time I could not hold it any longer. I had to speak up. So, out of my mouth followed aggressively, *"Stop it!"*

Shock covered her face. Almost like she had seen a ghost, she went pale and froze. I think that I must have been just as shocked.

Finally, I started to find some words. These words surfaced from me, and once I said them, I could no longer take them back. In a strained yet calm voice, I spoke to her firmly. I explained to her that she could never lay a hand on me again. I also explained that she will have to change her approach towards me moving forward and respect me when I say no. She would have to give me space when I needed it and if she could not do this, then we could no longer be friends. I do not remember the exact words I said, but I do know that she listened like it was an authority figure speaking to her. I do know whether I addressed the hitting, nudging and slapping and whether I said that would not accept any of that anymore.

She took this discussion as an end to the friendship. Everyone on the bus was consoling her as she would not stop crying the rest of the way home. I was tingling all over feeling flustered, but I could not take back the fact that I was standing up for what was right. No one should be touched inappropriately or abusively. No one should be forced to do anything against their own free will, even if the person is someone they adore or admire.

Control can be so ugly in relationships. It can destroy love and kindness and trust. In this instance, I learned how to address an issue in a friendship, but I also lost trust in people.

I never told anyone about the hardships in this friendship and the bullying that went on in private. I do believe some people witnessed the violence, but what followed did not address the inner issue. It just stopped the bullying from continuing. I did not really learn how to address control in my life. Instead, I began to protect myself from any people who might be wired this way. I became a floater or social butterfly, avoiding any deeper relationships with anyone in case they tried to manipulate or control me. I ran in the opposite direction from anyone of whom I thought were trying to control or push their views onto me. I valued my safety and guarded myself carefully. Without knowing it, I had built high, solid walls around my heart and found loneliness to be my only friend.

Now, guarding our hearts and minds against incorrect or negative influences is not at all bad. It is wise to guard and protect your heart and mind from influences that will tear you down.

When you avoid trusting anyone and run away rather than building deeper relationships, then something is not right. I avoided trusting any relationship by pushing people far away and the consequence was that I found loneliness to be my partner for a long time.

In my final year of school, the principal singled me out in the hallway. She eyeballed me and said, "You can do whatever you want after school is finished. You can be whatever you want to be. You do not have to follow anyone but you. You make the choice."

I reflected on these words that day and have continued to reflect on them over the years. These words penetrated through walls of chaos. I recognised that the principal was addressing my future choices for study and career but ultimately, she was highlighting the freedom of choice I held, any choice. The thought that developed over time was that I was *free* to make my own choices. For too long, I had time and again allowed control to take place in my world. I had allowed control to occur because I did not value myself.

Putting others before ourselves does not mean that we drive ourselves further down into a negative, hurtful place. Taking away any worth from ourselves does not build the value in others. If you have no value for yourself, what are you going to give to others?

Just imagine, you have a family to feed. Now think about the nice meal you would like to prepare and the selected drinks to complement the food in addition. Think about the delectable dessert to be wowed over and to be eventually devoured. Consider the time and money you need to finance the groceries needed for at home, and the logistics of getting it all there. Think about the table setting and the space you would like to present the meal in, picturing the kitchen and utensils needed for every part of this preparation. Maybe consider the decorations you would like to add to make it more special, or maybe you would like to light the fireplace, or add to the view and other various surroundings around you. Now picture yourself doing all of this while you are having an incredibly sore back; it's so bad that you cannot bend or even stand or move.

How could you ever prepare a meal for whoever you've pictured when you are unable to walk? How could you even think of making it special like that? I give this example because truthfully, despite our love for those around us and our best intentions, we often treat our hearts like they can overcome any issue and hurt without proper attention and care. If the issue is physical, we would have to see a doctor to help us function, or we would take temporary solutions to fix the issue like resting up. We cannot care for our loved ones if we are not physically well.

To best give from our heart and minds to the people we love or in general, we have to be healthy in our hearts and minds, too. Control destroys a part of ourselves as it takes something healthy about our personality and knowingly crushes it. When this happens, take your time to heal. It is OK to let yourself recover just like you would if you had a sore back.

As your own person, you can stay on a path of discovery and achievement; you should not have to hide what is occurring in your life to help the other person feel value. To have healthy relationships without control, we have to be able to give and receive. Therefore, continue to exemplify and lavish love, trust, kindness, loyalty, and whatever other values you encompass, to the people around you.

Control devalues the worth of a person, almost portraying them as being beneath any positive experience or love. Control steals the identity of a person; it stamps out their ideas and actions. Control hurts and destroys a person, because it restricts their freedoms and cages them in. Control eventually sucks the life out of a person. Control is at work when there is a lack of freedom to act as yourself or if you are unable to stay true to your inner being and personality because of the fear of someone's response.

However, people were never designed to be controlled. We were designed to be free.

So, how do we overcome control? There are four steps that

really helped me, and I believe they will help you, too:
- Recognise the signs;
- Seek help;
- Address the issue;
- Have clear boundaries.

Recognise the signs

As a teenager, I only realised things were not right when I was already in the middle of all the bullying, being physically hurt. I recognised that I was not allowed to be myself because of the issues my friend had with her inner self. I allowed her to control me because I loved her and our friendship. The fear of doing something wrong in her eyes made me hesitant about sharing what I thought or how I felt with anyone at school. As an adult, I did not recognise the effect of control until things had become really dark and dangerous. I could no longer be myself around anyone. I did not show my true self anymore for fear of being berated, ridiculed and yelled at in private. Only after this, I realised I could only be myself around certain friends who would call out the façade when they saw it.

Control happens subtly and can occur with people that we love. It is easy to tell a stranger to move on or to move away if they try to control us, but when we love someone this can create a way for compromise in this area. People can be easily mistreated because they love someone so dearly.

Control often happens for numerous reasons as we all have our own personalities and histories. Some people have not encountered healthy relationships and only know negatively geared relationships. Perhaps the only behaviour modelled to them has been manipulation and control. Perhaps they have had to live up to high expectations, and they were rebuked for their lack of achievement. Others find themselves entangled in control from a relationship that initially seemed healthy, but slowly changed into a cage without them being aware of it.

Having an understanding of what control is, what it does, and how to process the effects of it, can enable you to overcome such barriers in relationships to bring positive interactions and perhaps restoration. To recognise when our inner self is being stomped out, scared into submission, or caused to question self, whether it is through family members, friends, work colleagues and the lack of action to try. This becomes evident to the people around us first, and if they truly care, they will say something. Please, acknowledge it if you are not free to have a choice or speak or have an opinion.

Are you able to express yourself freely? Are you afraid of someone's response to you, fearful that they will ridicule or despise you or even hurt you? Are you afraid of being left behind or rejected for having an opinion of your own or for standing firm in a belief?

Recognise these signs of control around you. This is the first step to overcoming control.

Seek Help

It can be hard to question what is occurring in our relationships. Confrontation is uncomfortable, it is easier to try and ignore things and find an escape rather than to be honest about what is happening.

It can be hard to share the private on-goings in a relationship for fear of breaking trust or facing the shame of allowing something negative to go on for so long, or for allowing it to occur in the first place. There are many reasons for avoiding any issues in our lives, but with help we can progressively and successfully conquer the negative issues affecting a relationship. This can allow for growth, longevity, and a bright future in our relationships.

I think of it like a child who starts school and for the first time encounters the diversity of the classroom. Culture, personality, rules, values and beliefs. The child has to face everything alone, to begin with, but they are not alone in dealing with it. When a child learns new things, whether it is positive or negative, afterward a parent would usually ask questions about these new experiences. Through directed conversations of accountability and trust, the parent can guide the child to celebrate victories, overcome difficulties and recognise the positives and negatives within life.

In the same way, as adults we can also have wise counsel or help. This section has the heading "seek help" because like the innocent and immature child who is learning daily and seeks help from their parents, we too are learners in life. Life continues to evolve and change, expectations and desires continue to grow, and as resilient beings, we learn throughout our life. As learners, we benefit from the help around us like friends or family or professionals who keep us accountable regarding positive and negative influences within our world.

Just because we are adults, does not mean we have to process anything we face alone. When we have trusted relationships, we can find help to identify positive and negative circumstances, specifically regarding control. It can be more evident to others than to us. Parents, friends, colleagues, siblings, cousins, roommates can all witness the deterioration of a person's personality and presence. An outside perspective can see past emotions and feelings, they can call out the truth in a sea of mixed thoughts that can cloud judgment.

I remember when my separation was about to hit the five-month mark, I met with the celebrant who married us. This was an incredibly confronting moment, I felt like a complete failure and was not sure what to say. I sat with him and his wife in their living room and cried, asking for a way to bring our marriage together. He carefully and lovingly reassured me that this part was not up to me but to my ex-husband. Of course, I cried more, thinking I would do anything and yet it was not up to me. With conviction and caution, he also shared what he had witnessed in our relationship, he saw the control that had occurred from when we started dating to when we were married with a child. He saw that I had become a shell of the person I was. It was interesting how he used the terminology and tone of voice, while describing what I had become. To be told this, and know that I allowed it to happen, really frustrated and hurt me.

If I had not met with this celebrant and sought his help, he may not have had the confidence to say anything. Many friends also came forward sharing what they saw after I was free of my marriage or at least the control from the marriage, but during the marriage itself no one would say anything. I think if we only had some wise counsel to hear us both out along the way, perhaps we would have handled the circumstances differently and more positively. If we only had asked for help back then.

Having wise counsel and help throughout life is not about breaking trust but rather living a positive life with people who want to contribute to you and build you up to be the best version of you. You choose who this inner circle can be. Please, friend, find the people you can trust to help you through life. People who can laugh and cry with you, who are not afraid to be honest with you, who are trustworthy and build you toward a positive resolution. If you are a person of faith, hopefully you include someone who can pray with you and for you.

Address the issue

The amount of effort and awareness to an issue can be daunting, and can be extremely painful. There are reasons why things have been pushed down deep and buried for another day. Sometimes it is so much easier to run far away from the issue than to address it head-on.

Yet, we know the truth. If we face up to what has been encountered inwardly this will help in our self-growth and understanding.

If, instead of dealing with them, we keep shoving issues down, one on top of the other, we begin to harden our hearts. Just like hard rocks or clay within soil that terminates any healthy growth in a garden, it can be very difficult to grow a new or current relationship out of a hard heart. With issues upon issues in place, out of that heart will come words that demolish life.

Without addressing issues, the heart will stay hard, and eventually, these issues will surface and hurt you all over again because you have not even been given the chance to process through any of it. We have to acknowledge that these circumstances are hurtful, but they should not go on hurting us forever.

Who would want to live like that? We need to address the issue in order stop the hurt!

Addressing the issue will take time and focused effort. You will have to push through the pain and keep the end goal in front of you. Eventually, you will gain enough strength to overcome such grief, and you will learn to effectively accept whatever happened and to forgive, releasing you from the pain. Finding the root of the issue and addressing it, will ultimately empower change in the circumstance and a healthy resolve.

A large support to addressing issues is having the correct support network around you to help strengthen you when you are at your most vulnerable. Support networks can appear in different ways or formats. They can look like listening to positive podcasts on self-growth and personality, reading self-help books to build your inner self and, of course, participating in support groups whether sports networks, faith building groups, book clubs or any other positive social group with a purpose.

Having support while addressing the issues in life enables extra strength when we begin to grow weak. It can be hard to be vulnerable again after such trauma; but, have courage and step out in faith that you will be free of such burdens.

I remember when I had to address the issue with my ex-husband. We were standing in the kitchen and he was aggressively criticising my cooking when I offered him a plate of dinner. This occurred early in our separation period, while I was trying to piece our marriage back together. At the time, I thought I would make him dinner and we could chat together, but it backfired badly. Usually, I would have accepted the stern lecture and tried cooking again with him stressfully watching over my shoulder, shouting out comments every few minutes. I would then feel the pressure crushing me from all sides. But this time, after having filled myself with extra support and strength, I addressed the issue. I simply addressed that he did not have to eat it and that the aggression was unnecessary. I said this quite calmly; then he blushed and walked away. Addressing the issue empowers you to prevail in future circumstances and can liberate you from the root cause.

Have clear boundaries

After recognising the manipulation woven into my relationship and addressing the issue, there was a need to protect the freshly formed, healthy emotional state. Boundaries in relationships can be viewed negatively, but they do not always have to be like that.

Boundaries can protect and secure something precious inside an area, so that no unwanted attention can hurt or steal it away. Boundaries guide outsiders or onlookers to view the precious commodity without touching, damaging or engaging past a point of permission. Boundaries give both owner and onlooker a perspective on how to treat what is being carefully safeguarded. Boundaries highlight the value of the protected asset, ensuring clear-guided directions on how to care for such a priceless thing.

For instance, galleries protect and display art on the walls or stands on top of postured stilts. After paying a fee, you can wander about the gallery at your leisure. When walking these galleries, considerations are taken to remember the unspoken rule: "Do not touch any art." If there is an art piece that holds significant value, it usually has a glass box covering it and rope barriers around it to keep people further away. The gallery may also require an employee or security guard who ensures no one breaks any of the rules like moving under the rope barriers. Sometimes clear signs are placed around the artwork, entailing instructions not to touch anything or to cross under the barrier. The higher the value of the artwork, the more thoroughly it will be protected.

With this example of clear, intentional boundaries around a valuable art piece, we too should have clear and intentional boundaries to our hearts and our freedom. We, like the unique artwork, should have specific boundaries in place to guard our hearts against control and other issues that take place in relationships. Consider the required sacrifice, the vigorous effort, and the countless hours of time that the artist applied while creating something of value. It should be guarded well because of its worth. In the same way, after all the perseverance to recognise the issues buried deeply in our hearts and the massive effort to resolve them, why would we allow someone to penetrate the safe boundaries just for them to destroy the progression we painstakingly made? Having boundaries in place allows future love to blossom from the heart. Personal boundaries exhibit the value you have for yourself. Boundaries allow the heart to have the freedom to be unique and help others to respect individuality.

Having safeguards in place is not always easy. When in love, we should lower our guards, and sometimes our boundaries become more like guarded gates. We trust others to enter with care and concern. Having boundaries does not mean we avoid everyone or never allow someone to go past the boundary. As we trust again and relationships are restored, some loyal and trustworthy people can enter these boundaries.

I am still learning about who to let in. I know that my son enters as he pleases, without either of us even knowing it. I have found that loving someone beyond myself, can allow them to enter as they please. I have learned with others I love that, when hurt occurs between us, those boundaries almost light up in my mind. I see that I may have crossed past their line or vice versa. The vital discussion that follows ensures that a healthy relationship can continue. If these boundaries are not respected or communicated, it can be hard to have a healthy relationship that develops and thrives. Each unique person has different needs and should communicate them. A mutually respectful and loving relationship would consider these boundaries *and value them.*

Chapter 15
Moving Forward: Respect and Resilience

*T*hat did not just happen, did it?

It was always bittersweet for Matt and me when we would journey to my ex-husband's home. The apartment block was quite elegant and located close to appealing cafés and convenient shops. The three-story contemporary apartment belonged to his partner. I would encourage Matt to have a positive attitude and remember that he would see me soon. On the inside, I was reminding myself that I would see Matt soon, too, as the goodbyes also hurt my heart. I found that encouraging him to be positive would ultimately help both of us in the transition, benefitting our situation in the long term.

As per usual, Matt's dad happily collected him at the drop-off point outside the apartment blocks. As Matt kissed me goodbye and reached for his bag, Matt's dad politely thanked me for dropping Matt off. Matt was climbing out of the car with his low-spirited demeanour and dejected frown. Matt's dad would try to tickle him or tease him out of this mood, and I would try to leave as they were laughing. Yet, this time, Matt's dad casually proceeded to invite me in for dinner and drinks with Matt... Stunned, I found myself completely stunned. Taken by surprise, I stuttered something inaudible.

How is it after all these months of pleading to think of our marriage, hoping and wishing that he would change his mind about breaking up, that he would now do this? Into his *partner's* home? Did *she* know this? Was it a cruel joke to her or me? Was he planning something, or was he just going with the flow? What were the motivations and/or intentions behind the question?

I found myself so shocked and caught off guard at this question that I choked on my answer. "That is not appropriate. See you next time." I found the rising heat on my cheeks alarming, and I was so nervous that he noticed the bright crimson shade lighten my face. He then understood immediately that there was something wrong with what he asked. Briskly embarrassed he acknowledged my response and said nothing further. Matt yelled goodbye again and I waved, quickly driving away.

Was I perceiving this situation correctly? Did he think it was OK for me to enter his partner's home without her permission or knowledge, as she was absent? Was he thinking of Matt or of himself or both? I was so confused. I felt wronged and like I was almost used for some dark purpose. If I had said yes, I could have seen Matt for a longer time, but I would not be honouring his partner. I thought if I were her, I would want to know if my partner was having dinner with his ex. My reaction rose from the negative history between us, knowing how incredibly degrading and distressing it felt to have an unfaithful partner. Deep down, it was the obvious choice to leave and not go in, though confusion still followed.

Sometimes our desire to be accepted or loved can surpass what is right. Perhaps our perceptions of what we deserve for ourselves can override our morals and ethics. This selfish nature can happen over time, especially in today's society. When pondering this memory, feelings of anger at the potential injustice flooded my mind, for my dignity and worth, but also that of the partner of my ex. Shortly after, another feeling crossed my mind in relation to this memory that opposed the former. It was a feeling of rightful possession.

Let me explain this. This was my husband. That was my child. At the time, we were still married, only separated. I could spend a night having dinner with my family and nothing else would happen. After all, we had said vows and created this family, so I could very well do as I pleased, right? I could have told myself and anyone who asked that I do not owe anyone any explanation.

I know we can feel various feelings of control, resentment, or frustration when someone, or something, is taken from us. However, by trying to manipulate or control what is now gone, we can damage ourselves even more, as well as others around us. We can even become like the person or thing that hurt us in the first place. Reacting from unforgiveness and revenge will only create more complications and grief.

I am surprised that some strength was left in me to say "no". "No" to hurting this man and woman the way they had hurt me. "No" to lowering my standard of living just because he had the title of "husband" when in reality he no longer was that to me. I had to say "no". It was an act of love for all the people involved: my ex, his partner, Matt, and myself. I was neither going to change who I was nor my heart of love just because someone had hurt me. I chose to act in love even when I would be tempted with acts of revenge and hate.

So… Why was I confused? Admittedly, I wanted my marriage back, I still loved this man and truly *wanted* us to be a family again. I was confused because I wanted to go in, but I wanted a relationship that would last, a relationship with trust, integrity, and faithfulness. If I would begin this path with dishonour and lies or betrayal, I knew I would be unhappy in the long run because I would become what I stood firmly against. Just as I had been betrayed, now I did not want to be the cause of betrayal.

It took strength to say "no" in this situation. This was the first time that he asked me into their home, although there were multiple invitations to go for a drink or a date. He invited me in! The strength to decline came ultimately from the overflow of words of worth that flooded my mind from those who cared about me. *I am grateful for the people who persevered with me and reminded me of my worth.* If I did not understand how valuable I was, perhaps I might have made a choice that I would regret to this day.

Whatever you want to call this exchange: a chance, an opportunity, an invitation, a game? This could have ended multiple ways but to protect the future, I had to decline. There was no way he was ready to make a fresh start, he was still in a relationship with someone else. There had to be a choice on his part and mine. He wanted to dabble in both opportunities. That is not what I thought a trustworthy and faithful relationship entailed. It is definitely not what I wanted.

Choices like this can shape a person, but also affect the timeframe and desired nature for healing, restoration, and gained respect. Sometimes it is one step forward, two steps back. I share this story to illustrate how we can easily go back to the negative and degrading circumstances in our lives just to feel appreciated and accepted. But deep down, we know that doing so will tear us apart. Making these positive choices, despite that it can be excruciating, *will* benefit everyone involved. Forgiving ourselves for our mistakes, we can choose to see the potential future, driving positive change and the growth of our inner strength. When you know your value, there will be an unconditional expectation to respect this value by others and yourself.

Think of it like this. You have saved for a long time to finally be able to buy your dream car. Finally, after years of saving and hard work, you can now purchase the car, in the exact colour you like, with every add-on possible to make the car more desirable and luxurious. You can even have personalised plates. Immediately, a loving sibling or friend who does not have the greatest record for driving and taking care of cars, who has accidentally crashed or scratched every car they have owned, asks to borrow your car for a week, maybe a day, or even just for an hour. How easily would you lend this dream car out? How long would you entrust the prized possession to someone who you know would mistreat or damage it? You would consider the possible outcomes, costs for repairs, loss of transport, loss of your own use as it will take time to fix it.

A car has value, but once bought its value begins to depreciate. A car could never compare with the human heart. How much more value does our heart have? A value that never depreciates but ever increases?

I want to encourage you that your heart is valuable and should be treated like a treasure. Allow yourself to be open to those people who are willing to give of themselves. Protect your heart from those who do not appreciate it. Acknowledge those who do. Say "no" to the bait of short-lived pleasures, when you could gain a lifetime of self-respect, love, and self-worth.

It was a hard moment in my life to say "no" to the man I loved. A part of me thought that maybe I could win him back, but the rest of my senses shouted, *"At what cost?!"*

I was reminded of what true love meant to me. Love is kind and patient. Love is sacrificial and faithful. Love never gives up, never loses faith, is always hopeful, and endures through every circumstance. I lived by a love that was loyal, trustworthy, and committed. I could not become the opposite of what I believed love to be, to merely gain illusory love.

One Foot Forward

I am not a person who likes to shop, or spend, or use retail therapy to help supplicate my emotions. I am more of a budgeter and shop off the list type person. Yet, when Matt went to his dad's place as per the regular agreement, I could not tolerate sitting at home alone or conducting conversations with anyone. Honestly, I could not stand to hear any voice including my own, so I created a regular habit of distracting myself every week. There was no constructive work or play occurring but vacant wandering around a shopping centre. This attempt to distract my mind from the chaos that was brewing inside me was difficult, like pushing through an incline on a run. Holding back the tears was even greater; I was definitely a crier.

The distraction helped me to maintain some composure when I was out of the house, busying the mind with some task to do. I could not meet with others who knew of my situation as they would tend to ask directed questions, and that would release the flood gates of tears. I must have looked so gloomy and empty strolling the boutiques. I remember crossing paths with friends and acquaintances, and the conversations were strained. There was an unspoken understanding that I was distracting myself. Perhaps I was escaping the new reality that had formed?

Attempting to move forward, it seemed that the past would pop up and, as previously stated, it had to be dealt with. What was the root cause? Why did it bother me or Matt so much? Why am I reliving all this again?

During this period, Matt grew extremely angry, more so than any developing toddler. The boy was unsure of who to blame, and I could see he wanted me to save him. When this did not change, he would release his emotions by lashing out to me. There were hundreds of crossovers laced with heart-breaking, aggravated emotions, and sadly the response given to Matt was that of the court order restrictions. We were powerless to the law and had to submit.

It was difficult to face Matt, his dad, and his family members. *Everyone* had a say about what would be best.

At the time, the legal advice to us was to come to a mutual agreement outside of the court. It would avoid large costs, and it would help in rebuilding respect between both parties. I was afraid of losing my relationship with Matt's dad and losing Matt altogether. There was some common ground that should satisfy everyone, right?

In reflection, I know we have come such a long way, but to be reminded of how horrible those days were still shakes me now. The fear was greater than any good that could be done. The guilt in my head weighed heavily when Matt would leave, causing my heart to ache in ways nothing and nobody could soothe. I would feel this helplessness creep up inside of me, my throat grow dry, my stomach painfully rumble and quake, and my limbs begin to numb. I thoroughly understood that shattering feeling of failing my responsibilities as a mother who was supposed to be bold and courageous for justice of their child. My emotions certainly did not help me here. I had to find a place of calm, resilience and determination to help my son. The circumstances were not changing, but we could. Somehow, Matt and I would become stronger and wiser, and grow in resilience, patience and understanding to the circumstance we had to live in.

So, to move forward, we worked toward a partnership with Matt's dad in raising Matt and living this lifetime together but no longer in the same home or family. How do we respect one another? How do we interact with one another? We applied the timeless principle: "Treat others how we would want to be treated." It started with Matt and me being the persons we would want to live with, and by living out that example.

I think back to the marathon runner and their journey to success. The finish line is one part of the runner's success. The increase in strength, stamina, discipline and focus are other parts of their success; the improved change is success. I know that, in the same way, my son and I have become strong, perseverant, focused and disciplined in life despite challenges that occur and have occurred. We have learned—and still are learning—to live by example and lead our lives in love and peace despite the association, atmosphere and circumstance around us.

In those moments when Matt and I struggled to give time to his father, I recognised that we were stuck in this emotional turmoil. It was a negative cycle that just hurt us both. I found myself crying out, "There has to be another way!" Now it is easy to stay here and complain, perhaps fight a little, complain some more, and then give up. For my son and me there still was verbal abuse and manipulation that continued to control our inner being, even though there was a separation in families. I was allowing myself to be a slave to the fear inflicted over the years and I could not protect my son with this mindset. It was horrible!

The marathon runner has to persevere and refocus to reach the next level in their success cycle. To move forward, there is always a way. I knew this to be true for us as we began to change our mindset and re-adjust our focus.

Although the fear was present, I kept reminding myself and my son that there was always hope to move forward. To do so, I simply had to set one foot in front of the other. This was some of the best advice given during such a hard time in life.

I would be crying over the future, worrying over finances and legal fees, and sleep deprivation had become the norm. Even though my mind struggled to focus, I made a list of things that needed to be done. I prioritised the list and then acted day by day the best I could. I showed grace to myself when things were not completed that day and rewarded myself for any successes.

Before I knew it, I was moving forward even though emotionally I was incapable of comprehending any future. With the celebration of the successes, I also grew in confidence and boldness to take on the next step. It is like the marathon runner running the entire distance after months of walking parts of the course.

Accordingly, I learned to model, teach and be transparent with my son in how to work through emotions. Like in a relay race, I passed on the baton of forgiveness and perseverance to him, knowing that he would learn to move forward with his dad present in his world. This was the ideal future for us, although for now it was not easy. The goal was to run the race of life with fulfilment and joy, not to just reach the finish line. Matt would benefit knowing his dad loved him and together they, in their own way, would support one another in a loving relationship.

It was up to Matt to learn how to move forward in his way, but my duty is to give him the best chance to become the best version of himself. This included facing issues and circumstances in a healthy and proactive way.

Occasionally, Matt's dad would pick him up for a night or two, but mostly "forgot" or simply failed to show up. There was never an apology. Neither was there any communication on whether he was taking Matt for the weekend or weekday. Friends and family would urge me to report this behaviour to the court, but I could not bring myself to do it. I tried to be merciful, as I hoped our relationship would mend with peaceful resolutions rather than aggravated penance.

These years of mistreatment and disrespect reared rejected emotions that occasionally surfaced. I tried my best to limit this vulnerability to the safe and trustworthy people who would remind me of *my agreement to myself* to move forward. These trustworthy people did not encourage me to stay in the negative, but they highlighted the need to keep pushing forward.

With this, I am thinking of a coach. If a runner had a bad day of eating during their training period for a marathon, the coach would not join them in eating the burger and fries. Oh, no! The coach would reprimand the runner and then remind them of the goal and of the need to succeed. We may fail or fall off the path, but our coach, our support network, helps us back on the path to keep moving forward.

Whenever it suited him, Matt's dad would see his son and claim his rights. Early on, he would use nasty language, antagonise me, raise his voice with aggression and intimidation, and approach with a disgusted demeanour. I have to say that I was terrified at the meeting points every time, having to face such hatred. No matter the time or place, I ensured we met publicly. I promised myself that I would never be alone with him for fear of physical hurt as well as emotional suffering. I reflect now at those past moments in time and see that I was really treated like a doormat. But you know what? I did not lose. The negative treatment and communication came from a place deep within Matt's dad, that only he could resolve.

I had to ask myself what was my end goal for Matt, for Matt's dad and for me every time that we saw Matt's dad? Where did I want to be with Matt and his father in the future? What did I want Matt to have in the future?

I wanted Matt to have a positive relationship with his father.

I wanted to have a positive relationship with Matt's father. If possible, I wanted to – reconcile with him.

I wanted Matt, Matt's father, and myself to be happy, free of fear, anger and past negativity.

I wanted Matt to learn from both his mother and father.

Being constantly reminded by friends and family members that Matt needed a father, I visualised a guided path in my mind to ensure that Matt's father would be present for the overall good of Matt. Although by law Matt had to see his dad, I hoped that Matt would also genuinely connect and love his dad, and that his dad would accept and love his son. We constantly work on our mindsets to ensure we are growing and adjusting to life in the most positive and beneficial way.

Distraction, running away or avoidance does not help us move forward, though they seem easy to live by. To move forward we must face the pressure and hardship, with support.

Take that step, one foot in front of the other.

Write down action points that are relevant to your circumstance. Consider everyone involved, whether your child(ren), ex-partner, family members, friends, colleagues etc. Think about the time frames of discomfort or challenge or negativity. Think about the root cause of this challenging circumstance.

Now ask yourself, *what are some solutions here?*

Who helps in the circumstance, or who can help? When is this happening? And is there any way that you can ease the time frame of discomfort? For example, I had someone in the car when I dropped my son off to his father. Do you need to react, or can you walk away and allow time to prove the matter wrong? What is the root, and can you find a solution? Can you address the issue with the person involved? Can you bring in a mediator?

Share these action points with your support crew. Allow them to encourage you to stick to these positive and proactive steps, and to tweak them if you need to. This way can be an even better support to you on your journey of *forgiveness and healing*.

Chapter 16
Partnership as a Blended Family

*W*hat matters?

The question I had to ask myself daily is, what matters now?

I was fighting for a healthy, committed relationship and family. I was doing everything in my will power to maintain the peace, keep things in order and allow life to be the best it could be given our circumstances. I really was trying to do my best. With tears in my eyes, I would grit my teeth and ask for wisdom to move forward. It hurt to press forward but I knew that there was always hope.

What matters?

As I said before, I was fighting for something.

I think of the training involved for a fight. The daily ritual of eating specific foods to build lean, strong muscles, and to warm up and stretch to keep the adjoining ligaments of the muscles agile. There is the strenuous work of the muscles that sometimes breaks them, rips them, and then, the healing strengthens them to prevail in the most testing times. How a fighter grows stronger and more agile and fit, is quite incredible. They have a vision. They keep that vision in their sight every time training is tough. Every time they just want a sleep in, they remind themselves of the vision. Every time they desire a glass of their favourite beverage or treat, what will they do? Where are they going? Their vision on the desired outcome allows them to persevere through the struggle.

Connecting back, I had to keep what mattered in front of me. I had a vision for our relationship and family dynamic. I was fighting for a healthy, committed relationship and family. This could still be achieved, though the relationship status had changed. I could have a healthy relationship with Matt's dad. I could have a healthy family. Still, I had to consider what mattered more: was it justice, or was it revenge? Was it my rights? Was it Matt's rights? What was it?

I did not have a direct answer because of the overwhelming emotions flooding my entire being. I was bombarded by the hurt and the shame. I stayed there, in that dark, tormented place, until my son began to cry for attention.

He was so upset his world had been tipped upside down. He could not see his mum every day and he could not see his dad every day. His dad was there only so much, and the atmosphere in this relationship had changed. His mum was present but also absent at the same time; the atmosphere here was definitely different to what it was before. To this innocent little child his safety had been taken from him, his stability had been shaken, and the love we had for him was now in question. I was internally and externally crying all the time, or

I was attempting to escape the majority of those days, because the immensity of the hurt was crippling me. But my son was attached, and he would not let go.

One day we were sitting on a hill near our house and Matt was rolling down the hill and laughing with glee. I was deep in thought and would occasionally laugh with him, but I remember looking at the sky and thinking, "What matters now?" Meanwhile, Matt was on his way up the hill, and he veered toward me. He quickly grabbed my face with his tiny hands and looked me in the eyes. He made me focus on him. Then he asked me to roll with him, saying that he wanted to do this together.

This shifted my focus.

I was so embedded in self-pity, hurt and turmoil. I was dwindling away without recognising what matters. My child, thankfully, called me out of that moment, and absolutely I rolled down the hill with him almost daily from that point on until he grew out of it!

That moment was a turning point for me. I believe Matt was contributing to a consistent divine message that was being communicated to me throughout this circumstance. Multiple conversations and posed scenarios, and family and friends pointed to what matters. In my workplace, at my church, in my thoughts, this question was crossing my path and challenging me: what matters?

This was a profound realisation, what matters to us will drive us and motivate us to act. Whatever the need is, the path will lead toward meeting that need. The challenge is, what if that need is something negative or to be feared? Could it be detrimental to our health, whether physical or mental, founded in hate, driven by hurt? How many times will we hurt ourselves, or how many loved ones will be hurt along the path?

Those who suffered were myself along with my immediate family: my son, mum and dad. There were some friends that were collateral damage, too. I look back and I am grateful that these people lived by true love and grace. Even my son. They all forgave me in my rawest and rudest form, empathising with me and showing grace every time I snapped or blamed or rebuked anything said or done.

When I recognised what mattered in life and that it was founded in love, I could change my perspective and focus.

Instead of hate, I chose love.
Instead of confinement, I chose freedom.
Instead of revenge, I chose grace.
Instead of complaining, I chose gratefulness.
Instead of negativity, I chose to be positive.
Instead of shame, I chose to re-establish my identity
Instead of guilt, I chose to forgive myself.
Instead of inner torment, I chose to speak life and truth.
Instead of blame, I chose to pave the future path in honesty and commitment to be better.
Instead of comparison, I chose to own everything about me and work on myself.

What mattered to me was being a better me; a better human being on this planet, a better parent, friend, employee, servant, child, sibling, cousin. No one else was responsible for me. Only I was responsible. I was responsible to stay the best me despite what is thrown at me or whoever tried to take me down. I understood the ownership of who I was going to be on this earth and then acted upon it.

In this I am now thinking of building a house. The house firstly requires a solid foundation with firm grounding. The framework on top of this foundation is the skeletal struc-ture that supports and shapes the home, built with heavy-duty wooden beams and other related components to secure the frame to its foundation. You have the roof that is designed to repel and reflect heavy weathering and to protect the inner parts of the house. You have the interior and exterior design and functionalities.

The foundations of the home can relate to our own founda-tions that have formed and developed over our childhood, young adult years and adulthood. Culture, upbringing with our own parents, family, education and belief systems form the foundations of who we are. The foundations outwork into our dreams, desires, attitudes and mindset.

These mindsets, developed beliefs and dreams can relate to the framework of the house. Beliefs can relate to our response to any given situation, the way we protect ourselves and others, and how we approach the world. If we disagree, our mental protectors come up and stop the words, knowledge, material, or people that can take an unwanted effect on our foundations, our belief systems, or on our framework, our mindsets and dreams. This is not a negative thing. We protect our inner being and true self, and our value, by guarding what goes inside. The foundations and framework of who we are can change and, again, that is not a negative thing. This can be quite positive, especially when you invest into your mind and wellbeing with resources that strengthen and build your positivity.

Yet, we can lose sight of some of our foundational life prin-ciples because we have allowed something damaging to pene-trate our protection, our roof. Just like a massive hailstorm breaking through the roof surface and damaging the interior of a house, hurt can penetrate our protective strategies and start to damage our internal wellbeing.

We would call for a repairman to fix all the damages to a house and seal the roof so that no other leaks happen. In the same way, after we have learned to forgive and have processed the hurts, we secure our hearts and minds to avoid such pain again by learning from the process. After this, we also need to check the foundation and framework to confirm if there was any damage.

This highlights the importance of what matters in life. If a framework beam is damaged it can affect the entire structure, weakening the strength for future blows.

In the same way, we may lose sight of a principle we live by like kindness or honesty because of the hurt caused upon us. Or we may say, "I can never trust again because they broke my trust." Having the damage remain weakens us for future opportunities and relationships. It changes our approach and action.

Just as the house is repaired well and restored to functionality, so too our inner being and inner health can be restored to renewed health and functionality. And perhaps, a learned outlook on life can benefit for a brighter future.

What matters, I believe, is the foundation and the framework of who we are, not what may come to destroy it.

Out of this realisation, I learned to forgive no matter what. I learned to focus on life-giving circumstances and people. I learned that my life can change, depending on where my focus is. I learned I can be a life giver rather than a life drainer. I can be the example of what I was searching for. I can firstly give this out, to then influence my atmosphere around me, and receive it in turn. I learned that I can speak life and positivity into my environment. I can change my approach and attitude even if the circumstances remain the same. I can be the victor even when the victory is delayed, even where I was once the victim.

You are the victor. Choose to be the hero of your story every day.

It can be difficult to hold onto the frustration while you are around the atmosphere of forgiveness. It shifts a person's inner being when they are proactively acting in forgiveness and kindness. I have witnessed multiple people journeying through this process in their trauma, and it's incredible to see how either they are repulsed by the notion of letting go, or they take it in.

The common observation spoken over me was that how free I am despite the circumstance. I know it was such a relief when I let go, to forgive and to care despite how others were behaving. Even when people were repulsed by the idea of forgiveness and said some hurtful things about me, I could not hold onto any of it. I would wish them well and express to them respectfully, that I have chosen my path and it is beneficial for my future. I knew what forgiveness did for me. I would not change the process I was walking and now am living.

Thank God, He led me to learn this art. It not only has freed me from past hurts and traumatic experiences, but the art of forgiveness has taught me to continually practise forgiveness like breathing. For I make many mistakes and hope for forgiveness from others. Deep in my heart I never want to hurt anybody, but I am still a human being on a consistent learning journey. I learned very quickly that if I want to see a change in the environment that I work and live in, it must start with me.

The act became an art, there was focus, determination and vision of the destination. The time, the effort, the commitment and the humility throughout was consistent even if it was in small steps, and the vision was being acted upon in every word and deed. Do we want relationships that last? Do we want unity? Do we desire true love that fights for one another?

With these questions in mind, perhaps think about areas where pride has stopped a process of forgiveness and uniting a relationship that could have been saved. It may be confronting, but with time relationships can be saved.

Here I am thinking of those past relationships that I would say "never again" to; could the circumstances have been processed, communicated, or maybe even supported in a better way? What role did I play in this relationship? And if we crossed paths again, would I hide or would I say hi? Would I hope to leave the past behind and wish them well? I hope I will do this every time.

Please note, if you find yourself in an unsafe relationship, please don't get me wrong with the meaning to stay and wait till things resolve. Please, seek out safety measures first to keep you and your dependants safe.

In life, there will be people in various phases of their journey, whether they are processing their past hurts or not, and we will have some sort of an exchange. Whether it is in friendship, work relationships, religion, parenting, university etc. There are multiple ways to do life and most include interacting with other human beings. I hope that you now have an understanding that the art of forgiveness can entwine in all areas of your relationships. Whether the other person ever admits or understands their part, your part is to release and find freedom; this you can achieve if you act upon it.

Finished but partnered

It's all over. Yet the unwanted interactions continue, there is a strange partnership that is taking place. There are strong emotions present. There are multiple views from all sides of this village of people raising a child, and, somehow, I am desiring unity for our blended family.

How can this work?

When a relationship starts, there is consideration of two very different and unique people, from different backgrounds, experiences and cultures, uniting together as a couple. We know that when two come together, levels of kindness, patience and grace need to be applied to various relationship priorities like communication, respect, trust and selflessness.

In the same way, a broken relationship requires an agreement between both parties to work together. To partner together again from my end, I told myself to show grace and be the example. With every aggravated response, I owned my responsibility, I addressed the inappropriate behaviour, and respectfully made suggestions. When possible, I would be encouraging. The basic principles to a relationship needed to be rebuilt like trust, respect, kindness and patience.

Now, to take a step back...

There was that time when the information for my son's custody was presented to me and it was so confronting and alarming, that I felt totally overwhelmed and lost. This was the place where I desperately needed clarity and I needed truth.

Hearing hopeful scenarios, "what ifs", or short-term actions to take did not bring any clarity or truth to calm my depths of despair. I had to find *truth*. I started with what would come next. For me, the solicitor made everything clear about moving forward for the next two to five years. I still remember crying every time I received communications from the courts; it felt so unfair to me, and I just wanted to crawl into a quiet, small place and be left alone. I also thought of fighting for my rights and for custody. The hours of drafting, the stress incurred from continuous tension, the lack of finance and turmoil everyone faces through the process of it all; it again was so overwhelming. I remember many times asking people to stop talking about it all, to *just let me be*.

This was not a reality I could stay in, nor was it helpful to anyone around me. My son would suffer even more, my family and friends would suffer, and yes, I would suffer. I had to engage in this new parenting partnership to stop this continued suffering.

However, partnering with someone who had broken trust and respect with something or someone of incredible value was extremely difficult to me. How did I do this? How do we do this?

After hearing the hard truths and weighing up the choices at hand, I decided to honour the role I was given. I am a mother, I am one part of a partnership in parenting, and I am human. It is OK to have emotions and deep feelings. However, I had to take responsibility for myself and my interactions moving forward. I wanted to move on and, therefore, I did not want to stay the victim, but I wanted to be the victor. So, I had to believe that to own it. To act on that belief in order to gain this new identity, is what defines this part of the process: belief and identity.

Belief

Firstly, I had to believe it was possible to partner again with the father of my child. Belief is such a powerful thought process that can enable a person to act and achieve. It can set a person on a positive trajectory and even though they face hurdles and hardships, they will persist through every challenge because of their belief.

May I remind you of the athlete who is training for the marathon? If they believe they can achieve a specific goal, they will put the hard work in to achieve this. If there is a lack of belief, the training and consistency will lack with as an outcome any lack in results.

In the same way, if we believe that a relationship can be restored, we are half-way there. Every day, we can remind ourselves of what we are believing for. Anytime a hurdle arises, we need to believe that we will see what is envisioned come into existence, and we need to keep pushing through the hardship with gritted teeth.

The thoughts of reconciliation and restoration will lead to positive action toward a successful partnership of parenthood. Even when the other person is resistant, continued belief can enable change, growth and learning for future circumstances.

I think of how unsafe I felt every time there was an encounter with my ex-husband. Yet, when I began to believe again for a partnership that could benefit my son, things began to shift in my mind.

I chose to marry and love Matt's dad. He had many great characteristics that I would look for in a lifetime partner and the father of my children. Even though mistakes were made, the chance for that good man to surface again, and live up to his potential, remained. If he could achieve this, Matt would have a great father and would have more of a positive upbringing than with a father who was not present or in a hard place. Now, this was not my responsibility, but if there was a partnership based on mutual respect, then I could at least add positivity and growth. Matt would benefit. I would benefit, because my son was finding peace in some of the closest relationships around him.

This is where I found belief shifted our relational setting. I believed Matt could have relationship with his dad, and I taught him principles to be a respectful, forgiving and loving son. Matt is on that learning journey, but many times Matt has mentioned how his dad makes him laugh or helps him learn or gives bear hugs. Matt has acted on forgiveness after regularly speaking it in his prayers and believing for change. He celebrates these changes with me frequently, and it moves our blended family forward.

The reminder for me in all of this, was that I was not the only parent of this child; he also has a father who loves him. My ex-husband's change in love for me does not negate from the love he has for his son. I had to separate this. His dad could make the choice to build a relationship with his son, and I could help in this or make it difficult.

The belief that I could partner here, was vital for any action that I needed to take. The body and heart followed on with the belief that ultimately it was possible.

You know, relationships can change, respect can be built, the interactions can be positive, the partnerships can be mutually respectful and can allow for continued communication. Trust can be built. Kindness can be shared. Not everything has to end in an argument. We can partner together even though we are not together or have had brokenness in the past. Belief is a choice. Action follows.

Secondly, I chose to believe that everything was in God's hands.

This can be really hard. I can hear the resisting thoughts coming like a flood. "What God?" "Where was God when things hit the fan?" "How can you believe, when things have not changed?"

For me, this man who hurt me is not God. I am not God, either. So, our choices toward one another, came from each other, from two imperfect human beings.

My circumstance was not resolved by the love of others or self, nor was it solved by escaping or running into it. I had to come to a place of trusting that something would go right or at least better, and that regardless someone would fully understand and care.

I already had a relationship with God; not religion but a relationship. There is love, trust, and hope. He first loved me.

In this place of unconditional love, I discovered that I was forgiven and accepted. I found that I could completely trust Him, as I listened and developed my relationship with Him. I was guided every step of the way by his gentle voice and my belief was actioned by a beautiful example set for me. Ultimately, I learned what forgiveness is through the relationship I have with God.

Identity

The other aspect to successfully and proactively partnering with someone was knowing my identity.

When I was truly aware of who I am and what I represent, it did not matter that I had to partner with another person who had values and beliefs different to mine. The fact is, my identity could not be affected by this partnership if I am actively cultivating a healthy belief system, environment and thought process.

This is a continued responsibility that we can own in our every day, no matter the influences around us. Identity is pivotal to positive and negative choices, growth in personal action and learning, and in acceptance.

Throughout life's journey, we will be faced with both positive and negative environments. Actions and behaviours vary between personality types, levels of resilience and patience, and from the ability to forgive and let go.

The beauty of our abilities as learners is that we can be strengthened, be prepared and gain wisdom when facing varying situations. We can strengthen and prepare our identities for what awaits, by learning who we are, what we stand for, our strengths and weaknesses, our values and our worth.

Sometimes we lose sight of how incredible it is to be alive and to add to the community around us, by just being ourselves. I would love to encourage you in this. If you are in an environment that is hurting you or causing grief, remember your value and worth. Your identity is not connected to any of these scenarios, but rather it has equipped you (or it will equip you) and strengthen you to be an overcomer and fighter for future circumstances and for others who also have to face such trials.

Recently I discovered that I love stories, books and movies that have a hero or heroine, who had to face incredible hardships but did not give up. I realised that what I loved was their clear sense of identity: they knew who they were and who they could be, despite the negative circumstances or people trying to pull them down.

Thinking of your story and what you're currently facing or, perhaps a friend or loved one facing a circumstance of turmoil and confusion, remind yourself of your identity, remind them of theirs. Who are you? Who are they? And if the circumstances are stuck surrounded by a negative influence, remember to build that identity strong.

Put in the positive and replace and overload the the negative with proactive growth and encouraging influences. This can be received through cultivating loving and respectful relationships and conversations, developing a personal relationship and connection with God, reading and listening to uplifting podcasts and audios on personal development, and having moments of mindfulness reflection.

Your identity's health relies on you proactively pouring in the things that help it grow strong and beautiful. Take ownership and do not allow anything to dictate its health.

Sow and reap

I have heard the saying "sowing and reaping" over the course of my childhood and teenage years, and it has been reinforced throughout confrontations, educational forums and conversations. The idea of positively sowing into a relationship is related to the positive process of planting a seed. How you treat the seed and nourish it affects its growth. Not being a green thumb myself, I watched my mum dry out seeds on the window sill, and I asked her why. She explained the process, but I just thought, why dry it out when we are just going to replant it and water it again? Listening to my mum and looking a little deeper into this, if a seed is not dried, it can develop mould, or pests may eat it because they like moist seeds. The protective layer around the seed can be easily broken if it is wet, this would not help in healthy germination, development and growth.

In a similar way, there are parts of our relationships that have to be carefully nourished and treated. Every person is unique, and human beings have differing personalities.

This concept of sowing and reaping encouraged me to invest positive action into the family dynamic between Matt's dad, Matt and myself. I asked questions and thought of actions to take to encourage our family to move forward.

Questions like:

- How can I successfully converse with mutual respect?
- How can we have a relationship that exemplifies honour and kindness for our son?
- What would be the benefits and consequences of applying positive regard for one another?
- Is this important or are my feelings more important?
- Is it worth my time and effort, if it's not reciprocated?

I had to weigh this up, I had to consider how important this relationship is. So... Yes, he is my ex-husband... Yes, he hurt me... Yes, I hope for justice... *but* we have a child together.

That was it for me. My son. He needed positive examples of relationships, especially both with his dad and with his mum. This boy was maturing with such powerful influences. I am a powerful influence. His dad is a powerful influence. As parents, it was our responsibility to raise this boy right. The process to positive relationship began with forgiveness, then it led to building trust and respect.

Thinking about the adverse effects of treating the seed incorrectly, and how it could be damaged or die, made me overtly aware of my actions and responses. Do we need to repay a hurt with a hurt, or control with a rebuttal? Do we have to fight for ourselves every time, or is there a more peaceful and uniting way to communicate, interact and partner together while implementing effective boundaries and respect?

We all know that we cannot change others, neither is it our responsibility, but we can change ourselves. Being affected by circumstances that were not changing, I worked on being my best self in the circumstance that I had walked into. I owned every part of what I was responsible for and constantly asked what I could do better next time. This shifted responses and communication, enabling an open and mutual forum to facilitate respectful discussion and positive actions to follow. Through my experience, I can see the enriched positive environment that has resulted from a change in my mindset and proactive action.

The change from the other parties involved has been miraculous, especially since there were these fixed mindsets with a set pattern of behaviour. I still find myself grateful when positive words, encouragement and agreement do occur between such relationships. It is possible to see such change in your relationships, friend. It starts with us leading by example or at least taking first steps to provide a better relationship with those we do life with.

Just like the harvest is affected by what seed we sow under what circumstances, we have to be aware of what can affect our relationships. Are we constantly criticising? Are we thinking of the next point to add, or are we rebutting something shared, rather than just listening? Are we encouraging the person who is speaking? Are we adding value in any way? Are we positive with our words? Are we reading the body language and timing of the receiver? Are we sharing too much, or too little?

Let me encourage you, as you intentionally sow good seed into your relationships, your will reap blessings from them. I think of a relationship with a child. If you let the television babysit the child, they will quote phrases, ideas and sometimes language from such shows or the internet that perhaps you have never spoken or heard before. Something is sown into their mind and spirit when they watch others. What is reaped is the language and attitude that follows. This is only a small example, but as a parent myself I have seen such behaviour and attitudes.

It can be really difficult to acknowledge what we are sowing into and whether it is the best choice for a positive future. I think of a chilli seed, the chilli plant can grow into a mild flavoured chilli and sometimes the plant can grow into a fiery pepper that you cannot even smell or touch without our fingers, eyes and mouth burning! Now if a seed can be planted, nurtured and grown into such a spice, how much more can we plant seeds of change in our worlds? We can tend to this garden of ours, allowing our choices to weed, prune, nurture, water, fertilise and transplant from smaller to bigger. Our choices really can plant seeds, weed out positive and negative influences, prune off negative thoughts, behaviours, actions. They can truly transform the garden of our life.

One thing is for sure, what you are sowing into your everyday is what you will eventually reap and receive. Why not take the lead in the areas of life that you want to change and choose to sow what you desire?

I desired respect in my relationship with my ex-husband, so I started with me. Every time we spoke, I asked for strength in prayer, and then listened to him and responded respectfully. I humbled myself; although I thought many times that I was right; although I thought that I sounded like a doormat; although people did not agree with my actions. I checked that I held my boundaries intact, that I maintained my self-respect and that I was caring for my well-being, but I still humbled myself in moments that did not effect that.

I now know the value of my self-worth, and no one can take away from that anymore. Therefore, sowing respect into this relationship was straightforward and necessary to change our negative into positive.

The first few months I noticed him shift from angry to confused, from hurt and vengeful to hurt and uncertain. It was quite incredible to see that, after a year, a person who was spouting horrible, hateful words began to watch what they said, and apologise for incorrect behaviour.

This only progressed further with encouragement, deliberate mutual respect and care for the other person. What was once destructive, dark, despised and detrimental to both of us, became constructive, encouraging, transparent and driven.

We found our focus: to raise a strong, positive, proactive, diligent, loving and kind boy. Both of us hope and work towards our son standing on our shoulders, achieving greater things than either of us and becoming a positive influencer of his world around him. To achieve the great for our son, we had to work together.

I know this principle of sowing and reaping can be successful. It may take time, perseverance and consistency, but the value of achieving the dream is so worth the effort!

Let me encourage you. As you sow into your relationships, you will also reap from them.

As I worked on healing and overcoming the trauma, I taught my son to also forgive and allow for healing to take place. This process of doing and teaching, or modelling and teaching, motivated and empowered me to accept change.

Not only was I learning to act on principles that were logical and ethical, but I was learning to teach and model what I was learning. The process of educating others, especially a toddler, was quite complicated and challenging.

The deep-rooted differences in someone's upbringing, social status, desires, morals and convictions, culture, and personality all play a part in understanding an educational piece of information. As I began to teach other people who were going through broken relationships from the aspects I had learned on my own journey, I would listen to the heart.

I would wait to see if the person was ready to ask questions or to cry out for help. From similar experiences or scenarios, we could find connection, empathy and, sometimes, a solution. It was encouraging to know that sharing experiences and learnings propelled healing and the urge to move forward. I became increasingly aware that I was not alone in my hurt and that countless people needed guidance and help. With this growth and newfound knowledge, I also recognised the need for humility.

Humility can be a difficult personality trait to live by. I needed to remind myself that I had hurt and wronged my ex-husband, too. I had to remember that everyone with the correct boundaries and counselling or professional help can become a safe and caring individual again. This was my prayer especially for my son. I did not want him to grow up without his father. It was tough to partner at first, but we both understood we needed to humble ourselves for our son.

We needed to place a greater reason or drive above ourselves, to achieve humility and then, act lovingly for the greater good. What is that reason? Can there be any? For our circumstance, it was our child.

Recalling these early days of wanting my son to know his father and yet wanting to run in the other direction at the thought of parenting with him, I made the choice to commit to the parenting relationship. Every day we made the choice to raise this precious boy as best we could together. I was held accountable by close friends and family to continually make the choice to partner with Matt's dad.

When you make the choice to step out of the hurt into forgiveness, keep yourself accountable. Choose the right people who will cheer you on and guide you back to the choice you have made. This can be applied to any choice, to allow a trusted source to know your direction and to ask you about it regularly. They may offer you advice, ask great questions and encourage you. The importance of accountability is that it urges you forward toward fulfilling your purpose and dreams.

Accountability can see you shift perspective, achieve your desired outcome and have support. This type of support helped me to stay focused on providing a safe, supportive and caring environment for Matt.

You know when you work really hard toward a goal and, when signs of accomplishment start to show, you feel excited and anxious? This seemed to be the strange conundrum in which I found myself. My son had started to accept the circumstance we were in. He learned to have respectful relationships with his dad and step mum, and to know that time will pass. He spoke about his relationships with love and happiness, and would share that he missed his father. I felt pain when he said this. I felt both excitement that he had a positive relationship with his dad and anxiety that he would want to be with his dad and not me.

And then I remind myself of *sacrificial love*.

My pride, self-worth and feelings needed to be put in their place. I was working towards building an overcomer, a positive thinker and a resilient boy who would grow into a loving and kind gentleman. Instead of running from dark circumstances, I hoped we could learn from them, and then help others to overcome. I wanted my son to stand on both his parents' shoulders, taking their strengths and learning from their weaknesses.

If I allowed my emotions and insecurities to rule these moments, my son would back-track on his growth. I applied humility every time my child mentioned anything that made me feel insecure or anxious. I remembered that I will always be his mum. If I do my best to love this child, I will be fulfilling my purpose as a mother. Success in this task is seeing my son grow. I also regularly reminded myself that sacrificial love is putting his needs above my own. I disciplined my selfishness so as to encourage *love for another.*

Chapter 17
Saved by Grace

In completing the journey you've taken with me, I have to say there has been an underlying pull that has led my spirit - like the gravitational pull we have toward the earth. This incredible force has drawn me to higher heights and deeper depths of understanding of myself and others. I have learned what love is and how to act in love.

What is this pull? It is Love. Real Love. Pure Love. I've never known a Love like this, that accepted me at my worst and best, that saw potential in me, that believed in me, that had chosen me before I even knew it.

When I knew for myself how loved I am, it did not matter what was done to me. This Love cancelled out the lack of love or rejection that I faced. I was able to step back up, as I was not alone and I was *fully,* unconditionally and irrevocably adored. Love like this is found in Jesus Christ. He found me suffering and personally met me in my brokenness. He empathised with me and guided me while walking every step to freedom. I discovered an even deeper love than I had known before, with patience, kindness and no judgement.

Love measured by the standards of human capability can have limits, be conditional and lack commitment. It can be challenging to trust someone when there are negative thoughts plaguing the mind and experiences that prove unfaithful and unloving. I could work through these fears knowing Jesus was with me.

The journey of forgiveness began with my need for forgiveness. I had wronged people. I had made really bad choices and I knew it was wrong. Instead of sitting in my guilt and shame, Jesus met me with love and grace. I felt I deserved punishment and judgement. I was punishing myself and judging myself. I was busy beating myself up. But the grace of God was so powerful in my life; I understood the freedom of being forgiven. I was set free from my prison sentence, and I was loved and accepted.

Grace is marked on my heart, and through grace, I found love to be greater than anything else. Thankfully Jesus led me in this. Giving grace to others and choosing to forgive is still hard. Jesus will gently remind me, that I was first forgiven by God, and therefore I can now forgive.

Here are a few definitions of love:
Love is patient.
Love is kind.
Love is unconditional.
Love is not selfish.
Love is sacrificial.
Love would lay its life down for its friend.

How do you define love? Does love matter to you? Has this been closed in your world because of various circumstances, failures, disappointments, sufferings, guilt?

Everyone is loved. You *especially* are loved.

You may not believe in Jesus and that's OK. For me, Jesus saved me every time life was messy and He set me free. It was his wisdom and love that led me through the fire. So many times, people came through my world like fresh wind on a hot summer day, and Jesus would encourage me to listen and hear what they had to say. It was a breath of fresh air, a welcomed comfort and peace in the turmoil of everyday life.

The love that I grew with guided me and helped me be the best I could be in this life.

Through this love, I was led to the concept and the art of forgiveness. It became an everyday practice because I was loved so incredibly. It became easy to do as I did not need anything in return. I was no longer ruled by emotions or feelings of myself and others. I was free, like a bird gliding on hot currents in the air. They don't need to flap their wings or use any energy. They just glide on the currents with their wings outstretched. It became effortless to release things, I understood that my freedom came from a place of true love and acceptance. The love was beyond any I had known and I had endless access to this relationship. I could deepen the relationship through time and commitment, and through it all Jesus continues to love.

Worth

Through a deeply hurt and rejected state, I was delving deep into negative emotions and moving towards depression. It was a steep dive, easy to keep falling and not stand up or even be pulled up. My family and friends were by my side, speaking love and truth around me. I had to listen, or I would keep falling. My son would reach for love and speak love. Again, I had to listen or keep falling. Eventually, after months of all the love and support around me, I *heard* what everyone was saying. I heard the *truth:*

I am a great mother.
I am a faithful and trustworthy friend, daughter, sister and mum.
I am capable, strong and intelligent.
I am resilient. I am an overcomer and victor.

These were a few of the affirmations I claimed over myself to build my self-worth. My father gave me beautiful scriptures that spoke directly to the lies that I was hearing in my mind. Let these now also be a blessing to you in your journey of regaining healing in brokenness, as you practice the art of forgiveness in your own life.

Truth: You are loved

Romans 8.38-39 (ESV)
For I am sure that neither death nor life, nor angels nor rulers, nor things present nor things to come, nor powers, nor height nor depth, nor anything else in all creation, will be able to separate us from the love of God in Christ Jesus our Lord.

Psalm 86.16 (ESV)
But you, my Lord, are a God of compassion and mercy; you are very patient and full of faithful love.

Psalm 36.7 (CEB)
Your faithful love is priceless, God! Humanity finds refuge in the shadow of your wings.

Truth: You are accepted

1 Peter 2.9 (ESV)
But you are a chosen race, a royal priesthood, a holy nation, a people for his own possession, that you may proclaim the excellencies of him who called you out of darkness into his marvelous light.

Truth: You are forgiven

1 John 1.9 (ESV)
If we confess our sins, he is faithful and just to forgive us our sins and to cleanse us from all unrighteousness.

Friend, I hope you can receive whatever you need from these reflections. I pray a blessing upon you on your journey of forgiveness and growth. I pray for protection, support and for you to find victory over tumultuous times. I pray you find freedom, true freedom, peace that passes all understanding and hope again.

May our Good Lord bless and keep you, may His face shine upon you and bring you peace.

www.ingramcontent.com/pod-product-compliance
Lightning Source LLC
Chambersburg PA
CBHW032057020426
42335CB00011B/379